TEACHER'S PET PUBLICATIONS

LITPLAN TEACHER PACK
for
The Catcher in the Rye
based on the book by
J. D. Salinger

Written by
Mary B. Collins

© 1996 Teacher's Pet Publications
All Rights Reserved

This **LitPlan** for J. D. Salinger's
Catcher in the Rye
has been brought to you by Teacher's Pet Publications, Inc.

Copyright Teacher's Pet Publications 1996

Only the student materials in this unit plan
such as worksheets, study questions, assignment sheets, and tests
may be reproduced multiple times for use in the purchaser's classroom.

For any additional copyright questions,
contact Teacher's Pet Publications.

www.tpet.com

TABLE OF CONTENTS - *The Catcher in the Rye*

Introduction	5
Unit Objectives	8
Reading Assignment Sheet	9
Unit Outline	10
Study Questions (Short Answer)	13
Quiz/Study Questions (Multiple Choice)	20
Pre-reading Vocabulary Worksheets	35
Lesson One (Introductory Lesson)	45
Nonfiction Assignment Sheet	47
Oral Reading Evaluation Form	50
Writing Assignment 1	48
Writing Assignment 2	64
Writing Assignment 3	68
Writing Evaluation Form	67
Vocabulary Review Activities	62
Extra Writing Assignments/Discussion ?s	59
Unit Review Activities	69
Unit Tests	73
Unit Resource Materials	103
Vocabulary Resource Materials	117

ABOUT THE AUTHOR
J. D. SALINGER

SALINGER, J. D. (born 1919). Although he is one of the most widely read authors in the English language, J. D. Salinger successfully kept himself out of the public eye for most of his career. His preference for seclusion made his life a matter of speculation among fans and his literary output a subject of controversy among critics.

Jerome David Salinger was born in New York City on Jan. 1, 1919. After studying at Columbia and New York universities, he turned to writing. His first short story appeared in Story magazine in 1940. After service in World War II his stories appeared regularly in The New Yorker magazine. Major recognition and a large following came with his novel, 'The Catcher in the Rye', published in 1951. This touching and humorous story about a rebellious teenager became a cult book among university students. It was followed by 'Nine Stories' (1953), 'Franny and Zooey' (1961), 'Raise High the Roof Beam, Carpenters; and Seymour: an Introduction' (1963). The last three are mostly stories about the Glass family.

Altogether Salinger produced 13 short stories and one novel. Some of the stories made use of his wartime experiences, as in "For Esme-With Love and Squalor" (1950). "A Perfect Day for Bananafish" (1948) concerns the suicide of veteran Seymour Glass. Salinger seemed at his best in dramatizing the lives of children. Much of his work concerns the lost innocence of childhood.

INTRODUCTION

This unit has been designed to develop students' reading, writing, thinking, and language skills through exercises and activities related to *The Catcher in the Rye* by J. D. Salinger. It includes seventeen lessons, supported by extra resource materials.

The **introductory lesson** introduces students to one main theme of the novel through the first writing assignment of the unit. Following the introductory activity, students are given a transition to explain how the activity relates to the book they are about to read. Following the transition, students are given the materials they will be using during the unit. At the end of the lesson, students begin the pre-reading work for the first reading assignment.

The **reading assignments** are approximately thirty pages each; some are a little shorter while others are a little longer. Students have approximately 15 minutes of pre-reading work to do prior to each reading assignment. This pre-reading work involves reviewing the study questions for the assignment and doing some vocabulary work for 8 to 10 vocabulary words they will encounter in their reading.

The **study guide questions** are fact-based questions; students can find the answers to these questions right in the text. These questions come in two formats: short answer or multiple choice. The best use of these materials is probably to use the short answer version of the questions as study guides for students (since answers will be more complete), and to use the multiple choice version for occasional quizzes. If your school has the appropriate equipment, it might be a good idea to make transparencies of your answer keys for the overhead projector.

The **vocabulary work** is intended to enrich students' vocabularies as well as to aid in the students' understanding of the book. Prior to each reading assignment, students will complete a two-part worksheet for approximately 8 to 10 vocabulary words in the upcoming reading assignment. Part I focuses on students' use of general knowledge and contextual clues by giving the sentence in which the word appears in the text. Students are then to write down what they think the words mean based on the words' usage. Part II nails down the definitions of the words by giving students dictionary definitions of the words and having students match the words to the correct definitions based on the words' contextual usage. Students should then have a good understanding of the words when they meet them in the text.

After each reading assignment, students will go back and formulate answers for the study guide questions. Discussion of these questions serves as a **review** of the most important events and ideas presented in the reading assignments.

After students complete reading the work, a lesson is devoted to the **extra discussion questions/writing assignments**. These questions focus on interpretation, critical analysis and personal response, employing a variety of thinking skills and adding to the students' understanding of the novel.

Following the discussion, there is a **vocabulary review** lesson which pulls together all of the fragmented vocabulary lists for the reading assignments and gives students a review of all of the words they have studied.

The **group activity** which follows the discussion questions has students working in small groups to discuss the main themes of the novel. Using the information they have acquired so far through individual work and class discussions, students get together to further examine the text and to brainstorm ideas relating to the themes of the novel.

The group activity is followed by a **reports and discussion** session in which the groups share their ideas about the themes with the entire class; thus, the entire class is exposed to information about all of the themes and the entire class can discuss each theme based on the nucleus of information brought forth by each of the groups.

There are three **writing assignments** in this unit, each with the purpose of informing, persuading, or having students express personal opinions. The first assignment is to express personal opinions: students tell about the person they would most like to be like (picking up on the phony/pretending/acting theme). The second assignment is to inform: students introduce their characters for the character project, set up the scene they will be performing, and also write a post-performance conclusion. The third assignment is to persuade: students persuade Holden that everyone is not a "phony."

In addition, there is a **nonfiction reading assignment**. Students are required to read a piece of nonfiction related in some way to *The Catcher in the Rye*. Most students will combine this with the reading they have to do for their character projects. After reading their nonfiction pieces, students will fill out a worksheet on which they answer questions regarding facts, interpretation, criticism, and personal opinions.

The **review lesson** pulls together all of the aspects of the unit. The teacher is given four or five choices of activities or games to use which all serve the same basic function of reviewing all of the information presented in the unit.

The **unit test** comes in two formats: short answer or multiple choice. As a convenience, two different tests for each format have been included. In addition there is an advanced short answer unit test for higher level students.

There are additional **support materials** included with this unit. The **extra activities packet** includes suggestions for an in-class library, crossword and word search puzzles related to the novel, and extra vocabulary worksheets. There is a list of **bulletin board ideas** which gives the teacher suggestions for bulletin boards to go along with this unit. In addition, there is a list of **extra class activities** the teacher could choose from to enhance the unit or as a substitution for an exercise the teacher might feel is inappropriate for his/her class. **Answer keys** are located directly after the **reproducible student materials** throughout the unit. The student materials may be reproduced for use in the teacher's classroom without infringement of copyrights. No other portion of this unit may be reproduced without the written consent of Teacher's Pet Publications, Inc.

The **level** of this unit can be varied depending upon the criteria on which the individual assignments are graded, the teacher's expectations of his/her students in class discussions, and the formats chosen for the study guides, quizzes and test. If teachers have other ideas/activities they wish to use, they can usually easily be inserted prior to the review lesson.

UNIT OBJECTIVES - *The Catcher in the Rye*

1. Through reading J. D. Salinger's *The Catcher in the Rye*, students will study the theme of illusion vs reality and the idea of things or people being "phony."

2. Students will demonstrate their understanding of the text on four levels: factual, interpretive, critical and personal.

3. Students will study characters, setting, conflicts, motivations, and symbolism.

4. Students will study one character's confusion and uncertainty as he experiences the process of "growing up."

5. Students will be given the opportunity to practice reading aloud and silently to improve their skills in each area.

6. Students will answer questions to demonstrate their knowledge and understanding of the main events and characters in *The Catcher in the Rye* as they relate to the author's theme development.

7. Students will enrich their vocabularies and improve their understanding of the novel through the vocabulary lessons prepared for use in conjunction with the novel.

8. The writing assignments in this unit are geared to several purposes:
    a. To have students demonstrate their abilities to inform, to persuade, or to express their own personal ideas
        Note: Students will demonstrate ability to write effectively to <u>inform</u> by developing and organizing facts to convey information. Students will demonstrate the ability to write effectively to <u>persuade</u> by selecting and organizing relevant information, establishing an argumentative purpose, and by designing an appropriate strategy for an identified audience. Students will demonstrate the ability to write effectively to <u>express personal ideas</u> by selecting a form and its appropriate elements.
    b. To check the students' reading comprehension
    c. To make students think about the ideas presented by the novel
    d. To encourage logical thinking
    e. To provide an opportunity to practice good grammar and improve students' use of the English language.

9. Students will read aloud, report, and participate in large and small group discussions to improve their public speaking and personal interaction skills.

READING ASSIGNMENT SHEET - *The Catcher in the Rye*

Date Assigned	Chapters Assigned	Completion Date
	1-4	
	5-9	
	10-13	
	14-17	
	18-21	
	22-26	

UNIT OUTLINE - *The Catcher in the Rye*

1	2	3	4	5
Introduction Writing Assignment #1 PV 1-4	Read 1-4	Study ?s 1-4 PVR 5-9	Study ?s 5-9 PVR 10-13	Study ?s 10-13 Character Project PVR 14-17
6	**7**	**8**	**9**	**10**
Study ?s 14-17 Library PVR 18-21	Study ?s 18-21 PVR 22-26	Study ?s 22-26 Extra ?s	Vocabulary	Writing Assignment #2
11	**12**	**13**	**14**	**15**
Group Activity	Reports & Discussion	Character Project	Character Project	Writing Assignment #3
16	**17**			
Review	Test			

P = Preview Study Questions   V = Prereading Vocabulary Work   R = Read

STUDY GUIDE QUESTIONS

SHORT ANSWER STUDY GUIDE QUESTIONS - *The Catcher in the Rye*

Chapters 1-4
1. Who is Holden Caulfield?
2. Where is Holden as he narrates the story?
3. Why wasn't Holden at the big football game?
4. Why wouldn't Holden be back to Pencey after Christmas vacation?
5. What "dirty trick" did Mr. Spencer pull on Holden?
6. Who was Robert Ackley?
7. Who was Stradlater?
8. Identify Jane Gallagher.
9. Why doesn't Holden go down to see Jane?

Chapters 5-9
1. About what did Holden write Stradlater's composition?
2. Why did Holden tear up the composition he had written for Stradlater?
3. Why did Stradlater hit Holden?
4. Where did Holden decide to go?
5. Who did Holden meet on his train ride? Why did Holden lie to her about Ernie?

Chapters 10-13
1. Who is Phoebe?
2. Identify Bernice, Marty and Laverne.
3. Describe Holden's relationship with Jane Gallagher.
4. Why did Holden have to leave Ernie's?
5. What do we learn about Holden from his diversion about his gloves being stolen at Pencey?
6. What was the "big mess" Holden got into when he got back to the hotel after being at Ernie's?

Chapters 14-17
1. Why did Maurice hit Holden?
2. Holden said he felt like committing suicide. Why didn't he?
3. Identify Sally Hayes.
4. Why did Holden check out of the hotel, and where did he go?
5. Who did Holden meet at the "little sandwich bar" after he locked his bags at the station? What did they talk about?
6. What record did Holden get for Phoebe? Why?
7. What made Holden "not so depressed anymore" on his way to the record store?
8. Why didn't Holden like actors?
9. Why did Holden like the museum so much?
10. What did Holden think of "George something--"?
11. How did Holden's feelings for Sally change from the beginning of the date to the end?

The Catcher in the Rye Short Answer Study Guide Page 2

Chapters 18-21
1. What did Holden think of the show at Radio City?
2. Why did Holden call Carl Luce even though he didn't like him much?
3. What did Holden and Luce discuss?
4. Why did Holden go home so early (before Wednesday)?
5. What was Phoebe's reaction when she first saw Holden? What was her reaction when she found out that he had been expelled?

Chapters 22-26
1. What was Holden's reply when Phoebe asked him why he "got the ax again"?
2. Identify James Castle.
3. Why did Holden go to Mr. Antolini's house?
4. Why did Holden leave Mr. Antolini's home before morning?
5. What advice did Mr. Antolini give Holden?
6. How did Phoebe surprise Holden? What was Holden's reaction?
7. Why did Holden sit on the bench in the rain even though it was coming down in buckets?
8. How did Holden explain his catcher in the rye daydream?

KEY: STUDY GUIDE QUESTIONS - *The Catcher in the Rye*

Chapters 1-4

1. Who is Holden Caulfield?
    He is the main character, the narrator telling us about the things that happened to him.

2. Where is Holden as he narrates the story?
    He is in a California rest home undergoing some treatment.

3. Why wasn't Holden at the big football game?
    He had just returned with the fencing team and he had to go see his history teacher, Mr. Spencer.

4. Why wouldn't Holden be back to Pencey after Christmas vacation?
    He has been kicked out because he failed four out of five subjects.

5. What "dirty trick" did Mr. Spencer pull on Holden?
    He orally read back Holden's exam essay answer and the note Holden had written to him, truly embarrassing Holden.

6. Who was Robert Ackley?
    He lived in the room next to Holden at the dormitory. He had a pimpley face and he didn't go anywhere often. Holden said he was nasty and thought he was a nuisance.

7. Who was Stradlater?
    He was Holden's roommate. Holden said he was good looking but conceited.

8. Identify Jane Gallagher.
    Jane lived next door to Holden before he came to Pencey. They played checkers together and became friends. One can tell he really liked her. Stradlater had a date with her.

9. Why doesn't Holden go down to see Jane?
    He wasn't "in the mood."

Chapters 5-9

1. About what did Holden write Stradlater's composition?
    He described his dead brother Allie's baseball glove, which had poems written on it in green ink.

2. Why did Holden tear up the composition he had written for Stradlater?
    Stradlater complained that it was about a baseball glove instead of a room or some more typical composition topic. He insulted Holden, so Holden ripped up the paper.

3. Why did Stradlater hit Holden?

    Holden got mad because of Stradlater's attitude towards Jane Gallagher, and he started calling Stradlater a moron. Holden threw the first punch in the fight, but Stradlater hit Holden in the face, knocked him down and gave him a bloody nose.

4. Where did Holden decide to go?

    He decided to leave Pencey early to go to a hotel in New York and wait until Wednesday to go home to give his parents time to get the letter from school and get over the fact that he has been kicked out of yet another school.

5. Who did Holden meet on his train ride? Why did Holden lie to her about Ernie?

    He met the mother of a school mate. He didn't like Ernie, but since his mother seemed nice, he wanted her to feel proud of her son and wanted to tell her what she wanted to hear.

Chapters 10-13

1. Who is Phoebe?

    She is Holden's little sister. He likes her a lot and apparently they communicate well.

2. Identify Bernice, Marty and Laverne.

    They were three young women from Seattle on vacation in New York. Holden met them and danced with them in the Lavender Room.

3. Describe Holden's relationship with Jane Gallagher.

    They seem to have been good friends, playing checkers and going to movies and talking. There was no advanced romantic involvement between them.

4. Why did Holden have to leave Ernie's?

    He met Lillian Simmons there and chatted with her for a while. Rather than sitting with her and her date for the evening, he told her he was just about to leave, anyway. Then he felt like he had to leave so she wouldn't think he was lying.

5. What do we learn about Holden from his diversion about his gloves being stolen at Pencey?

    We know he doesn't like to fight because he doesn't like to look at the other guy when he hits him. He calls himself a coward -- "yellow" -- but he is really just too humane to hurt someone else.

6. What was the "big mess" Holden got into when he got back to the hotel after being at Ernie's?

    The elevator operator, Maurice, set him up with a prostitute. When she arrived, he didn't want her services. They talked for a little while, then he paid her the $5 he owed her. She insisted the fee was $10. Holden refused to pay the extra $5.

Chapters 14-17

1. Why did Maurice hit Holden?
    Holden refused to give Maurice the extra $5 for Sunny. After Sunny had taken the money from his wallet, Maurice "snapped his fingers very hard on [Holden's] pajamas . . . . it hurt like hell." Holden called Maurice a dirty moron, so Maurice slugged him in the stomach.

2. Holden said he felt like committing suicide. Why didn't he?
    "I didn't want a bunch of stupid rubbernecks looking at me when I was all gory."

3. Identify Sally Hayes.
    Holden called her for a theater date for Sunday afternoon. "She gave me a pain in the ass, but she was very good looking."

4. Why did Holden check out of the hotel, and where did he go?
    He didn't want to meet Maurice again, so he checked out. He went to Grand Central Station and checked his bags in one of the lockers there.

5. Who did Holden meet at the "little sandwich bar" after he locked his bags at the station? What did they talk about?
    He met two nuns. They talked mostly about literature and Holden's thoughts about *Romeo and Juliet*.

6. What record did Holden get for Phoebe? Why?
    He bought "Little Shirley Beans" which was about a "kid who wouldn't go out of the house because two of her front teeth were out, and she was ashamed to." He liked it and thought Phoebe would, too.

7. What made Holden "not so depressed anymore" on his way to the record store?
    He heard a kid singing "If a body catch a body coming through the rye."

8. Why didn't Holden like actors?
    He thought actors were the biggest phonies of all.

9. Why did Holden like the museum so much?
    "The best thing, though, in that museum was that everything always stayed right where it was."

10. What did Holden think of "George something--"?
    He thought George was a snobby phony and resented his butting in on his date.

11. How did Holden's feelings for Sally change from the beginning of the date to the end?
>He started out saying he loved her and they talked of marriage. By the end of the date, he hates her and she hates him.

Chapters 18-21

1. What did Holden think of the show at Radio City?
>He thought the "Christmas thing" was phony and stupid, and the picture was "so putrid [he] couldn't take [his] eyes off it."

2. Why did Holden call Carl Luce even though he didn't like him much?
>Holden was desperate for a companion with whom to pass the time. He also thought that since Carl Luce was quite intellectual, Luce might be able to help him.

3. What did Holden and Luce discuss?
>They mostly talked about Luce's romantic life and Holden's lack of one.

4. Why did Holden go home so early (before Wednesday)?
>He wanted to see Phoebe.

5. What was Phoebe's reaction when she first saw Holden? What was her reaction when she found out that he had been expelled?
>At first she was glad to see him and gave him affectionate hugs. When she found out that he had been expelled, she said, "Daddy'll *kill* you!"

Chapters 22-26

1. What was Holden's reply when Phoebe asked him why he "got the ax again"?
>". . . A million reasons why. It was one of the worst schools I ever went to. It was full of phonies. And mean guys. You never saw so many mean guys in your life."

2. Identify James Castle.
>He was a student who happened to borrow a sweater from Holden. He committed suicide.

3. Why did Holden go to Mr. Antolini's house?
>He didn't want to stay at home, and he was out of money for hotels. It was really his last resort.

4. Why did Holden leave Mr. Antolini's home before morning?
>Because he woke up to find Mr. Antolini stroking and patting his head, he thought Mr. Antolini might be making advances towards him; he thought Mr. Antolini might be a "flit."

5. What advice did Mr. Antolini give Holden?
   "The mark of the immature man is that he wants to die nobly for a cause, while the mark of a mature man is that he wants to live humbly for one."

6. How did Phoebe surprise Holden? What was Holden's reaction?
   She had packed her bags to go with Holden and she said she would not go back to school. Holden told her she could not go with him, which made her angry. He later said he wasn't going anywhere, either.

7. Why did Holden sit on the bench in the rain even though it was coming down in buckets?
   He was enjoying watching Phoebe ride the carousel; it made him happy.

8. How did Holden explain his catcher in the rye daydream?
   "Anyway, I keep picturing all these little kids playing some game in this big field of rye and all. Thousands of little kids, and nobody's around -- nobody big, I mean -- except me. And I'm standing on the edge of some crazy cliff. What I have to do, I have to catch everybody if they start to go over the cliff -- I mean if they're running and they don't look where they're going I have to come out from somewhere and *catch* them. That's all I'd do all day. I'd just be the catcher in the rye and all. I know it's crazy, but that's the only thing I'd really like to be."

MULTIPLE CHOICE STUDY GUIDE/QUIZ QUESTIONS - *The Catcher in the Rye*

<u>Chapters 1-4</u>

1. Who is Holden Caulfield?
    a. He is a writer for a New York newspaper
    b. He is a sixteen year old student at a prep school in Pennsylvania
    c. He is a psychiatrist at a well-known hospital in California
    d. He is an up and coming movie star in Hollywood

2. Where is Holden as he narrates the story?
    a. He is at his parents' house in New York.
    b. He is on a plane flying to Europe.
    c. He is in the school library.
    d. He is at a rest home in California.

3. Why wasn't Holden at the big football game?
    a. He couldn't afford the ticket.
    b. He was on academic probation and was not allowed to attend any extra-curricular activities.
    c. He had just returned to school with the fencing team and had to see his history teacher.
    d. He had to finish a term paper that was due the next Monday.

4. Why wouldn't Holden be back to Pencey after Christmas vacation?
    a. He had been expelled because he failed four of five subjects.
    b. He had lost his athletic scholarship and could not afford the tuition.
    c. He had been given an early acceptance to college and was starting the next semester.
    d. His father was sick and he had to go to work to help support the family.

5. What "dirty trick" did Mr. Spencer pull on Holden?
    a. He orally read back Holden's exam answer and the note Holden had written.
    b. He had a surprise going away party, even though Holden had said he didn't want a party.
    c. He pretended to be dead to scare Holden.
    d. He called Holden's parents while Holden was present and discussed his (Holden's) situation with them.

6. Who was Robert Ackley?
    a. He was tall and athletic, with a good sense of humor.,
    b. He was fair-skinned and had a large birthmark on his right cheek. He was intelligent and friendly.
    c. He was short and heavy with a mean disposition.
    d. He had a pimply face. He was a nuisance and rather nasty.

The Catcher In the Rye Multiple Choice Study Questions Page 2

7. Who was Stradlater?
    a. He was Holden's English professor. He tried to encourage Holden to stay in school.
    b. He was the coach of the fencing team. He wanted Holden to pay for the lost equipment.
    c. He was Holden's good-looking, but conceited roommate.
    d. He was a shy boy who lived down the hall from Holden.

8. Identify Jane Gallagher.
    a. She was the sister of a boy on the fencing team. She usually attended the games, hoping to attract Holden's attention.
    b. She had lived next door to Holden before he came to Pencey. They played checkers and became good friends.
    c. He was the headmaster's daughter. Holden had been dating her until her father made them stop seeing each other.
    d. She was the daughter of his mother's best friend. Holden introduced her to Stradlater because he didn't want to date her himself.

9. Why doesn't Holden go down to see Jane?
    a. He wasn't in the mood.
    b. Stradlater threatened to punch him if he did.
    c. He didn't think she would remember him.
    d. He didn't want to get stuck taking her out.

The Catcher In the Rye Multiple Choice Study Questions Page 3

Chapters 5-9

1. About what did Holden write Stradlater's composition?
   a. It was about his bedroom when he was a little boy.
   b. It was about the inside of a New York subway car.
   c. It was about the shower stall between his room and the adjoining one.
   d. It was about his dead brother's baseball glove.

2. What happened to the composition Holden wrote for Stradlater?
   a. Stradlater turned it in and got an "A" on it.
   b. Stradlater insulted Holden about the topic and Holden ripped it up.
   c. The English teach recognized Holden's style and failed Stradlater.
   d. Stradlater didn't use it because Jane wrote one that he liked better.

3. Why did Stradlater hit Holden?
   a. Holden cursed at Stradlater for stretching out his jacket.
   b. Holden refused to turn the lights out and stop smoking.
   c. Holden called him a moron, and then threw a punch at him.
   d. It was Stradlater's way of showing that he didn't want Holden to leave the school.

4. Where did Holden decide to go?
   a. He thought he would go to California to see his brother.
   b. He decided to visit Jane Gallagher.
   c. He thought it best to go directly to his parents' house.
   d. He decided to leave Pencey early and stay in a hotel in New York for a few days.

5. Whom did Holden meet on his train ride? Why did he lie to her?
   a. He met a friend of his mother's. He lied because he was afraid she would tell his mother she saw him.
   b. He met the mother of a school mate. He lied because he wanted the mother to feel proud of her son, and he wanted to tell her what she wanted to hear.
   c. He met a friend who had graduated from Pencey the previous year. He lied because he was embarrassed to admit that he had flunked out.
   e. He met one of his teachers from elementary school He lied because she had always had a good opinion of him, and he didn't want to change that.

The Catcher In the Rye Multiple Choice Study Questions Page 4

<u>Chapters 10-13</u>
1. Who is Phoebe?
    a. She is Holden's little sister, who he likes a lot.
    b. She is an old friend of Holden's brother.
    c. She is Holden's aunt, in whom he confides.
    d. She is a playmate from his early childhood.

2. Identify Bernice, Marty and Laverne.
    a. They are three chambermaids in the hotel where Holden stays.
    b. They are characters in a short story Holden is writing.
    c. They are three women whom Holden met and danced with in the Lavender Room.
    d. They are Jane Gallagher's school friends. Holden met them in the hotel dining room.

3. Describe Holden's relationship with Jane Gallagher.
    a. They have been romantically involved for over a year, although they are currently having a disagreement because Jane wants to date others and Holden doesn't.
    b. They seem to be good friends, playing checkers, going to movies, and talking. There was no advanced romantic involvement between them.
    c. They used to be romantically involved but now they can't stand each other.
    d. They have only spoken a few times, but Holden would like to get to know her better.

4. Why did Holden have to leave Ernie's?
    a. They evicted him because he was underage.
    b. He rant out of money.
    c. He was drunk and felt like he was going to get sick.
    d. He didn't want to sit with his brother's friend and her date.

5. What do we learn about Holden from his diversion about his gloves being stolen at Pencey?
    a. He calls himself a coward, but he is really too humane to hurt anyone.
    b. He is very selfish and materialistic.
    c. He will jump at any chance to fight.
    d. Possessions don't mean a lot to him.

6. What was the "big mess" Holden got into when he got back to the hotel after being at Ernie's?
    a. He was drunk and lost his temper. He started destroying the furniture and punching holes in the walls in his room. The hotel security came to subdue him.
    b. He was being chased by a group of young boys. He ran into the hotel for safety and they followed him in. The management came to his rescue.
    c. He didn't have enough money to pay his cab fare. The cab driver followed him into the hotel and up to his room, complaining loudly that Holden had not paid.
    d. The elevator operator set him up with a prostitute, and told him the fee was $5.00. When she arrived, he decided he didn't want her services, and paid her the $5.00. She said it was $10.00, but Holden refused to pay the extra $5.00.

The Catcher In the Rye Multiple Choice Study Questions Page 5

Chapters 14-17

1. Why did Maurice hit Holden?
    a. Maurice was roughing Holden up to make him pay Sunny the extra fee. Holden called Maurice a dirty moron, so Maurice hit him in the stomach.
    b. Holden had made insulting remarks about the caliber of the hotel, the prostitute, and Maurice's job. Maurice didn't want to hear it from a teenager, so he hit Holden to shut him up.
    c. Sunny had lied and told Maurice that Holden had hit her. Maurice believed he was defending Sunny.
    d. Maurice was just a bully. He enjoyed roughing up the young rich boys.

2. Holden said he felt like committing suicide. Why didn't he do it?
    a. He wanted to write a letter to Phoebe first, but he didn't have paper or pencil, so he decided to wait.
    b. He was afraid he might not succeed, and then he would have to face his parents.
    c. He didn't want a bunch of "stupid rubbernecks" looking at him all gory.
    d. He was going to jump out the window, but he couldn't get it open. He got tired of trying, and fell asleep.

3. Identify Sally Hayes.
    a. She was the girl his roommate often dated. He was mad at Stradlater for going out with Jane, so he decided to get even by taking Sally out.
    b. She was the receptionist at the hotel. She saw that Holden was having some difficulties, and offered to call a doctor or one of his friends to help him.
    c. She was another girl who worked with Maurice. She tried to seduce Holden, but he wisely refused this time.
    d. She was a girl Holden sometimes dated. He didn't like to too much, but he thought she was good looking.

4. Why did Holden check out of the hotel, and where did he go?
    a. He was out of money, so he went to sit in the subway station.
    b. He didn't want to meet Maurice again, so he went to Grand Central Station and checked his bags in a locker there.
    c. Sally had invited him to spend the rest of the weekend at her parents' house.
    d. The heat broke down in the hotel, so he went to a YMCA and got a room there instead.

5. Whom did Holden meet at the sandwich bar? What did they talk about?
    a. He met Sunny. They talked about what had happened the night before.
    b. He met two nuns. They talked about literature and Holden's views on Romeo and Juliet.
    c. He met Stradlater. They talked about school and Holden's personal problems.
    d. He met Ernie, the piano player. They talked about Holden's brother.

The Catcher In the Rye Multiple Choice Study Questions Page 7

6. What record did Holden get for Phoebe? Why?
    a. He got "Little Shirley Beans." He liked it and thought Phoebe would too.
    b. He got "The Skaters' Waltz" by Strauss because it was her favorite skating song.
    c. He got Shirley Temple singing, "On the Good Ship Lollipop." Phoebe liked to pretend she was Shirley Temple.
    d. He got "The Twelve Days of Christmas," because he knew she had to learn it for the school play.

7. What made Holden "not so depressed anymore" on his way to the record store?
    a. He was energized by the lights and all of the activity on Broadway.
    b. He watched some jugglers and street mimes and they made him laugh.
    c. He hears a young boy singing, "If a body catch a body coming through the rye."
    d. He started praying and realized that praying helped him a lot.

8. What was Holden's opinion of actors.
    a. He said they were all snobs.
    b. He said they were morons who couldn't get decent jobs.
    c. He said they were jerks who only thought about money.
    d. He said they were the biggest phonies of all.

9. What did Holden like best about the museum so much?
    a. It was free on Sundays.
    b. Everything always stayed where it was.
    c. It reminded him of fun times with his parents and brothers when he was young.
    d. It was warm and cheerful, and no one bothered him.

10. What did Holden think of "George something--"?
    a. He thought George was nice guy, and he was glad to be rescued from Sally for a while.
    b. He thought George was better than him, and he was afraid he would lose Sally.
    c. He thought George was snobby, phony and resented him butting in on his date.
    d. He thought he and George would have a lot in common, and wanted to get to know him better.

11. Describe Holden's feelings for Sally at the beginning of the date and at the end.
    a. He started out by saying he loved her and they talked of marriage. By the end of the date he hated her.
    b. He didn't like her much at the beginning, but by the end he was in love and proposed to her.
    c. He liked her somewhat at the beginning, by the time the date was over he was in love.
    d. He didn't like her at first, and really hated her by the end.

The Catcher In the Rye Multiple Choice Study Questions Page 8

Chapters 18-21
1. What did Holden think of the show at Radio City?
    a. He said it was the best show he had ever seen.
    b. It was supposed to be religious, but he didn't think it was.
    c. It was phony and stupid.
    d. It was a comedy of errors.

2. Why did Holden call Carl Luce even though he didn't like him much?
    a. Holden was desperate for companionship, and also though Luce was intellectual and could help him.
    b. He wanted to borrow money. He knew Luce was rich, and was a sucker for a sob story.
    c. Luce has his own apartment. Holden wants Luce to let him stay with him until Wednesday, when he can go home.
    d. Holden knew Luce was an A student. He wanted Luce to tutor him over the holidays.

3. What did Holden and Luce discuss?
    a. They discussed Holden's career possibilities.
    b. They discussed Luce's romantic life and Holden's lack of one.
    c. They discussed books they had both read recently.
    d. Holden told Luce all about his adventures of the last few days.

4. Why did Holden go home so early (before Wednesday)?
    a. He decided the most noble thing to do was go ahead and face his parents.
    b. He was feeling very ill, and was afraid he would get worse if he didn't take care of himself. He knew his mother would care for him, even if she were angry with him.
    c. He wanted to see Phoebe.
    d. He knew they were out. He wanted to get food and cigarettes while they were gone.

5. What was Phoebe's reaction when she first saw Holden? What was her reaction when she found out that he had been expelled?
    a. She was glad to see him, and hugged him. Then she said their father would kill Holden when he found out.
    b. At first she was scared, because she thought he was a thief. Then she worried about what would happen to him if her parents came home and found him there.
    c. She was angry that he woke her up, and even angrier that he had been expelled.
    d. At first she was selfish, and asked if he had brought her a present. Then she got sarcastic and said their father was used to Holden being expelled.

The Catcher In the Rye Multiple Choice Study Questions Page 9

Chapters 22-26

1. What was Holden's reply when Phoebe asked him why he "got the ax again"?
    a. He said the work was too hard because he had not been adequately prepared at the last school.
    b. He said it was unfair, that the teachers just didn't like him and were out to get him.
    c. He said it was because the president of the school board and his (Holden's) father had a political disagreement. Holden was being expelled to get even with his father.
    d. He said it was one of the worst school he ever attended, full of phonies and mean guys.

2. Identify James Castle.
    a. He is the president of Holden's class at Pencey.
    b. He is a psychiatrist Holden had visited a few times.
    c. He was a student who borrowed a sweater and later committed suicide.
    d. He was a business associate of Holden's father. He had once offered to help Holden get a job.

3. Where did Holden go and why?
    a. He went to a nearby church. He though it would help him to talk to a minister, regardless of their denomination.
    b. He went to a former teacher's (Mr. Antolini) house. It was his last resort, because he was out of money.
    c. He went to see Jane Gallagher, to warn her about Stradlater.
    d. He went to the convent to see the two nuns he had met earlier. He wanted to talk to them some more about Shakespeare.

4. Why did Holden leave Mr. Antolini's home before morning?
    a. Mr. Antolini was having a wild party. Holden was afraid to get caught there if the police were called.
    b. Mr. and Mrs. Antolini were having a fight, and Holden didn't want to be caught in the middle of it.
    c. He though he could see Phoebe on her way to school.
    d. He woke up and found Mr. Antolini patting his (Holden's) head. He though Mr. Antolini might be making advances towards him.

5. What advice did Mr. Antolini give Holden?
    a. "Only educated and scholarly men are able to contribute something valuable to this world."
    b. "I simply find Eastern philosophy more interesting than Western."
    c. "The mark of the immature man is that he wants to die only for a cause, while the mark of a mature man is that he wants to live humbly for one."
    d. "You're a real prince; a gentleman and a scholar."

The Catcher In the Rye Multiple Choice Study Questions Page 10

6. How did Phoebe surprise Holden? What was Holden's reaction?
   a. She brought her mother along. Holden was secretly glad, although he did not tell her that.
   b. She had packed her bag to go with him. He told her she couldn't go, which made her angry. Then Holden told her he wasn't going, because he didn't want her to be angry.
   c. She packed a lunch for him and gave him the rest of her savings. He cried because she was so trusting and so good to him.
   d. She didn't show up at lunch time. Holden was upset that he wouldn't get to see her, but deep down he believed she made the wisest choice.

7. Why did Holden sit on the bench in the rain even though it was coming down in buckets?
   a. He was enjoying watching Phoebe ride the carousel.
   b. He wanted to get sick enough to have to go into the hospital for a while.
   c. He was drunk and didn't realize what he was doing.
   d. He was punishing himself for behaving so badly.

8. How did Holden explain his catcher in the rye daydream?
   a. He would be running through a field of rye and farmers with pitchforks would be chasing him.
   b. He would play baseball wearing his brother's glove, and stand in the outfield, ready to catch anything that came his way.
   c. He would stand guard over all of the rye whiskey in the world and make sure no one got drunk.
   d. He would stand in a field of rye, where his job would be to catch any children who started to go over the cliff.

ANSWER KEY - MULTIPLE CHOICE STUDY/QUIZ QUESTIONS
The Catcher in the Rye

Chapters 1 - 4
1. B
2. D
3. C
4. A
5. A
6. D
7. C
8. B
9. A

Chapters 5 - 9
1. D
2. B
3. C
4. D
5. B

Chapters 10 - 13
1. A
2. C
3. B
4. D
5. A
6. A

Chapters 14 - 17
1. A
2. C
3. D
4. B
5. B
6. A
7. C
8. D
9. B
10. C
11. A

Chapters 18 - 21
1. D
2. A
3. B
4. C
5. A

Chapters 22 - 26
1. D
2. C
3. B
4. D
5. C
6. B
7. A
8. D

PREREADING VOCABULARY WORKSHEETS

VOCABULARY - *The Catcher in the Rye*

Chapters 1 - 4 Part I: Using Prior Knowledge and Contextual Clues

Below are the sentences in which the vocabulary words appear in the text. Read the sentence. Use any clues you can find in the sentence combined with your prior knowledge, and write what you think the underlined words mean in the space provided.

1. . . . my parents would have about two <u>hemorrhages</u> apiece if I told anything personal about them.

2. The whole team <u>ostracized</u> me the whole way back on the train.

3. Do you have any particular <u>qualms</u> about leaving Pencey?

4. . . . he made us have <u>compulsory</u> study hall in the academic building . . . .

5. I started <u>groping</u> around in front of me, like a blind guy, but without getting up or anything.

6. I was pretty <u>sadistic</u> with him quite often.

7. It was very <u>ironical</u>. It really was. "I'm the one that's flunking out of the goddam place, and you're asking me to write you a goddam composition," I said.

8. All I need's an audience. I'm an <u>exhibitionist</u>.

Part II: Determining the Meaning: Match the vocabulary words to their dictionary definitions.

___ 1. hemorrhages   A. Getting pleasure from inflicting pain on others
___ 2. ostracized   B. One who likes to show off and get attention
___ 3. qualms   C. Bursting of blood vessels
___ 4. compulsory   D. Meaning the opposite of what is expressed
___ 5. groping   E. Shunned; excluded; left out
___ 6. sadistic   F. Reaching blindly
___ 7. ironical   G. Feelings of doubt
___ 8. exhibitionist   H. Required; must be done

Vocabulary - *The Catcher in the Rye* Chapters 5 - 9

Part I: Using Prior Knowledge and Contextual Clues

Below are the sentences in which the vocabulary words appear in the text. Read the sentence. Use any clues you can find in the sentence combined with your prior knowledge, and write what you think the underlined words mean in the space provided.

9. If you knew Stradlater, you'd have been worried, too. . . . He was <u>unscrupulous</u>.

10. It partly scared me and it partly <u>fascinated</u> me.

11. I'm not too tough. I'm a <u>pacifist</u> if you want to know the truth.

12. My grandmother'd just sent me a wad about a week before. I have this grandmother that's quite <u>lavish</u> with her dough.

13. It's not a paradise or anything, but it's as good as most schools. Some of the faculty are pretty <u>conscientious</u>.

14. Well, a bunch of us wanted old Ernie to be president of the class. I mean he was the <u>unanimous</u> choice.

15. . . . I don't want to stay at any hotels on the East Side where I might run into some acquaintances of mine. I'm traveling <u>incognito</u>.

Part II: Determining the Meaning: Match the vocabulary words to their dictionary definitions.

___ 9. unscrupulous   A. Attentive to duty; diligent
___ 10. fascinated   B. In disguise
___ 11. pacifist   C. Having no moral code; unprincipled
___ 12. lavish   D. Generous or liberal in giving or spending
___ 13. conscientious   E. Held the attention of; captivated
___ 14. unanimous   F. One who opposes the use of force under any circumstances
___ 15. incognito   G. Showing or based on total agreement

Vocabulary - *The Catcher in the Rye* Chapters 10 - 13

Part I: Using Prior Knowledge and Contextual Clues
　　Below are the sentences in which the vocabulary words appear in the text. Read the sentence. Use any clues you can find in the sentence combined with your prior knowledge, and write what you think the underlined words mean in the space provided.

16. The band was <u>putrid</u>. Buddy singer. Very brassy, but not good brassy--corny brassy.

17. . . . the whole summer long we played tennis together almost every morning and golf almost every afternoon. I really got to know her quite <u>intimately</u>.

18. . . . old Ernie turned around on his stool and gave this very phony, <u>humble</u> bow.

19. One thing I have, it's a terrific <u>capacity</u>. I can drink all night and not even show it, if I'm in the mood.

20. He got stinking, but I hardly didn't even show it. I just got very cool and <u>nonchalant</u>.

21. Do you mind getting me my <u>frock</u>?

Part II: Determining the Meaning　　Match the vocabulary words to their dictionary definitions.

___ 16. putrid　　　　　　A. Ability to contain, absorb, receive and hold
___ 17. intimately　　　　B. Rotten
___ 18. humble　　　　　C. Showing a lack of concern; casual indifference
___ 19. capacity　　　　　D. Coat; cloak
___ 20. nonchalant　　　　E. Privately, personally, very closely
___ 21. frock　　　　　　F. Lowly; unpretentious

Vocabulary - *The Catcher in the Rye* Chapters 14 - 17

Part I: Using Prior Knowledge and Contextual Clues
Below are the sentences in which the vocabulary words appear in the text. Read the sentence. Use any clues you can find in the sentence combined with your prior knowledge, and write what you think the underlined words mean on the lines provided.

22. . . . I'm sort of an <u>atheist</u>. I like Jesus and all, but I don't care too much for most of the other stuff in the Bible.

_____

23. . . . He picked them at <u>random</u>. I said He didn't have time to go around analyzing everybody.

_____

24. He was always saying snotty things about them, my suitcases for instance. He kept saying they were too new and <u>bourgeois</u>.

_____

25. She'd hand in her basket and then go someplace <u>swanky</u> for lunch. That's what I liked about those nuns. You could tell, for one thing, that they never went anywhere <u>swanky</u> for lunch. It made me so damn sad when I thought about it, their never going anywhere <u>swanky</u> for lunch or anything.

_____

26. . . . he was one of the biggest bores I ever met. He had one of those very <u>raspy</u> voices, and he never stopped talking, practically.

_____

27. He was with some gorgeous blonde, and the two of them were trying to be very <u>blase'</u> and all, like as if he didn't even know people were looking at him.

_____

Part II: Determining the Meaning   Match the vocabulary words to their dictionary definitions. If there are words for which you cannot figure out the definition by contextual clues and by process of elimination, look them up in a dictionary.

___ 22. atheist   A. Smug, conventional, materialistic
___ 23. random   B. Grating
___ 24. bourgeois   C. A person who believes there is no God
___ 25. swanky   D. Having done something so much as to be bored by it
___ 26. raspy   E. Expensive and showy
___ 27. blase`   F. Haphazardly; by chance

Vocabulary - *The Catcher in the Rye* Chapters 18 - 21

Part I: Using Prior Knowledge and Contextual Clues
    Below are the sentences in which the vocabulary words appear in the text. Read the sentence. Use any clues you can find in the sentence combined with your prior knowledge, and write what you think the underlined words mean in the space provided.

28. Jane said he wasn't a show-off. She said he had an <u>inferiority</u> complex.

29. The bartender was a <u>louse</u>, too.

30. He kept telling her she had <u>aristocratic</u> hands.

31. . . . I was careful as hell not to get <u>boisterous</u> or anything. I didn't want anybody to notice me . . . .

32. All of them swimming around in a goddam pot of tea and saying <u>sophisticated</u> stuff to each other and being charming and phony.

33. I have this one stupid aunt with <u>halitosis</u> that kept saying how *peace*ful he looked lying there.

Part II: Determining the Meaning   Match the vocabulary words to their dictionary definitions.

___ 28. inferiority   A. Noisy and unruly
___ 29. louse   B. Of an upper class; distinguished
___ 30. aristocratic   C. Bad smelling breath
___ 31. boisterous   D. Strong feelings of inadequacy
___ 32. sophisticated   E. A person regarded as mean or contemptible
___ 33. halitosis   F. Worldly wise; refined

Vocabulary - *The Catcher in the Rye* Chapters 22 - 26

Part I: Using Prior Knowledge and Contextual Clues
Below are the sentences in which the vocabulary words appear in the text. Read the sentence. Use any clues you can find in the sentence combined with your prior knowledge, and write what you think the underlined words mean in the space provided.

34. All they did with the guys that were in the room with him was <u>expel</u> them. They didn't even go to jail.

35. She gets headaches quite <u>frequently</u>.

36. And if the boy <u>digresses</u> at all, you're supposed to yell. "Digression!" at him as fast as you can.

37. Holden . . . One short, faintly stuffy, <u>pedagogical</u> question. Don't you think there's a time and place for everything?

38. Or you may end up in some business office, throwing paper clips at the nearest <u>stenographer</u>.

39. You'll learn from them--if you want to. Just as someday, if you have something to offer, someone will learn something from you. It's a beautiful <u>reciprocal</u> arrangement.

Part II: Determining the Meaning   Match the vocabulary words to their dictionary definitions.

___ 34. expel   A. Strays temporarily from the main topic
___ 35. frequently   B. Characteristic of teaching or teachers
___ 36. digresses   C. Interchangeable; complimentary
___ 37. pedagogical   D. Often
___ 38. stenographer E. One who takes shorthand
___ 39. reciprocal   F. Push out by force

ANSWER KEY - VOCABULARY
The Catcher in the Rye

Chapters 1 - 4
1. C
2. E
3. G
4. H
5. F
6. A
7. D
8. B

Chapters 5 - 9
9. C
10. E
11. F
12. D
13. A
14. G
15. B

Chapters 10 - 13
16. B
17. E
18. F
19. A
20. C
21. D

Chapters 14 - 17
22. C
23. F
24. A
25. E
26. D
27. B

Chapters 18 - 21
28. D
29. E
30. B
31. A
32. F
33. C

Chapters 22 - 26
34. F
35. D
36. A
37. B
38. E
39. C

DAILY LESSONS

LESSON ONE

Objectives
1. To introduce *The Catcher in the Rye* unit.
2. To distribute books and other related materials
3. To preview the study questions for chapters 1-4
4. To familiarize students with the vocabulary for chapters 1-4
5. To give students the opportunity to express their personal opinions
6. To give the teacher the opportunity to evaluate students' writing skills

Activity #1
Distribute Writing Assignment #1. Discuss the directions in detail, and give students about 30 minutes to complete the assignment. Collect the papers for grading.

TRANSITION: Ask students for some of their definitions for the word phony.
"In the book we are about to read, the main character, Holden Caulfield, thinks just about everyone is a phony."

Activity #2
Distribute the materials students will use in this unit. Explain in detail how students are to use these materials.

<u>Study Guides</u> Students should read the study guide questions for each reading assignment prior to beginning the reading assignment to get a feeling for what events and ideas are important in the section they are about to read. After reading the section, students will (as a class or individually) answer the questions to review the important events and ideas from that section of the book. Students should keep the study guides as study materials for the unit test.

<u>Vocabulary</u> Prior to reading a reading assignment, students will do vocabulary work related to the section of the book they are about to read. Following the completion of the reading of the book, there will be a vocabulary review of all the words used in the vocabulary assignments. Students should keep their vocabulary work as study materials for the unit test.

<u>Reading Assignment Sheet</u> You need to fill in the reading assignment sheet to let students know by when their reading has to be completed. You can either write the assignment sheet up on a side blackboard or bulletin board and leave it there for students to see each day, or you can "ditto" copies for each student to have. In either case, you should advise students to become very familiar with the reading assignments so they know what is expected of them.

<u>Extra Activities Center</u> The Extra Activities portion of this unit contains suggestions for an extra library of related books and articles in your classroom as well as crossword and word search puzzles. Make an extra activities center in your room where you will keep these materials for students to use. (Bring the books and articles in from the library and keep several copies of the puzzles on hand.) Explain to students that these materials are available for students to use when they finish reading assignments or other class work early.

<u>Nonfiction Assignment Sheet</u> Explain to students that they each will be doing some related nonfiction reading in this unit. Students will fill out a nonfiction assignment sheet after completing the reading to help you evaluate their reading experiences and to help the students think about and evaluate their own reading experiences.

<u>Books</u> Each school has its own rules and regulations regarding student use of school books. Advise students of the procedures that are normal for your school.

<u>Activity #3</u>
Preview the study questions and have students do the vocabulary work for Chapters 1-4 of *The Catcher in the Rye*. If students do not finish this assignment during this class period, they should complete it prior to the next class meeting.

NONFICTION ASSIGNMENT SHEET
(To be completed after reading the required nonfiction article)

Name _____ Date _____

Title of Nonfiction Read _____

Written By _____ Publication Date _____

I. Factual Summary: Write a short summary of the piece you read.

II. Vocabulary
    1. With which vocabulary words in the piece did you encounter some degree of difficulty?

    2. How did you resolve your lack of understanding with these words?

III. Interpretation: What was the main point the author wanted you to get from reading his work?

IV. Criticism
    1. With which points of the piece did you agree or find easy to accept? Why?

    2. With which points of the piece did you disagree or find difficult to believe? Why?

V. Personal Response: What do you think about this piece? OR How does this piece influence your ideas?

WRITING ASSIGNMENT #1 - *The Catcher in the Rye*

PROMPT

Sometimes when we read books or watch movies, a particular character will appeal to us. We think, "Gee, I wish I could be more like that person" or "Wow! Would I like to be that person--even for a day!"

Your assignment is to write a composition in which you tell what person you would most like to be like, describe that person, and tell why you would like to be like him or her. You may choose a character from fiction or a real person from the past or present.

PREWRITING

Maybe you know right away who you would like to be. Great! Write that person's name down on a piece of paper and skip to the next paragraph. If you don't have the slightest idea, grab a piece of paper and a pencil. Make a list of your favorite books, plays, movies, television shows, sports figures, television actors, and people in history. Next to the books, plays, movies, and television shows, write down the names of your favorite characters from each. You should now have a whole list of people's names in front of you. Simply choose the one you would most like to be like! Write that person's name at the top of a fresh sheet of paper (or on the back of the paper you've already started.)

Under your person's name, make three columns. In the left-hand column, make a detailed list of that person's physical characteristics: physical build, hair color and style, kind of clothing he/she wears, etc. On the middle column, make a list of that person's character traits: super-strong, really intelligent, bubbly personality, great sense of humor, etc. In the right-hand column make a list of reasons why you would like to be like this person.

DRAFTING

Write an introductory paragraph in which you introduce the idea that you would like to be like the person you have chosen. Follow that with one paragraph describing the physical and character traits of your person. Then, write one paragraph for each of the reasons you would like to be like this person. Then write one paragraph for each of the reasons why you would like to be like this person. Use a topic sentence to state the reason, and in the rest of the paragraph explain your reason using specific examples. Sum it all up with a concluding paragraph in which you bring together your ideas and bring your composition to a close.

PROOFREADING

When you finish the rough draft of your paper, ask a student who sits near you to read it. After reading your rough draft, he/she should tell you what he/she liked best about your work, which parts were difficult to understand, and ways in which your work could be improved. Reread your paper considering your critic's comments, and make the corrections you think are necessary. Do a final proofreading of your paper double-checking your grammar, spelling, organization, and the clarity of your ideas.

LESSON TWO

Objectives
1. To read chapters 1-4
2. To give students practice reading orally
3. To evaluate students' oral reading

Activity

Have students read chapters 1-4 of *The Catcher in the Rye* out loud in class. You probably know the best way to get readers with your class; pick students at random, ask for volunteers, or use whatever method works best for your group. If you have not yet completed an oral reading evaluation for your students this marking period, this would be a good opportunity to do so. A form is included with this unit for your convenience.

If students do not complete reading chapters 1-4 in class, they should do so prior to your next class meeting.

ORAL READING EVALUATION - *Catcher in the Rye*

Name _____ Class____ Date _____

SKILL	EXCELLENT	GOOD	AVERAGE	FAIR	POOR
Fluency	5	4	3	2	1
Clarity	5	4	3	2	1
Audibility	5	4	3	2	1
Pronunciation	5	4	3	2	1
_____	5	4	3	2	1
_____	5	4	3	2	1

Total _____ Grade _____

Comments:

LESSON THREE

Objectives
1. To review the main events and ideas from chapters 1-4
2. To preview the study questions for chapters 5-9
3. To familiarize students with the vocabulary in chapters 5-9
4. To read chapters 5-9

Activity #1

Give students a few minutes to formulate answers for the study guide questions for chapters 1-4, and then discuss the answers to the questions in detail. Write the answers on the board or overhead transparency so students can have the correct answers for study purposes. Note: It is a good practice in public speaking and leadership skills for individual students to take charge of leading the discussions of the study questions. Perhaps a different student could go to the front of the class and lead the discussion each day that the study questions are discussed during this unit. Of course, the teacher should guide the discussion when appropriate and be sure to fill in any gaps the students leave.

Activity #2

Give students about fifteen minutes to preview the study questions for chapters 5-9 of *The Catcher in the Rye* and to do the related vocabulary work.

Activity #3

Assign students to read chapters 4-7 of *The Catcher in the Rye* prior to your next class period. If there is time remaining in this period, students may begin reading silently.

LESSON FOUR

Objectives
1. To check to see that students read chapters 5-9 as assigned
2. To review the main ideas and events from chapters 5-9
3. To preview the study questions for chapters 10-13
4. To familiarize students with the vocabulary in chapters 10-13
5. To read chapters 10-13
6. To evaluate students' oral reading

Activity #1

Quiz - Distribute quizzes and give students about 10 minutes to complete them. (Note: The quizzes may either be the short answer study guides or the multiple choice version.) Have students exchange papers. Grade the quizzes as a class. Collect the papers for recording the grades. (If you used the multiple choice version as a quiz, take a few minutes to discuss the answers for the short answer version if your students are using the short answer version for their study guides.)

Activity #2

Give students about 15 minutes to preview the study questions for chapters 10-13 and to do the related vocabulary work.

Activity #3

Have students read chapters 10-13 orally for the remainder of the class period. Continue the oral reading evaluations. If students do not complete reading these chapters during this class period, they should do so prior to your next class meeting.

LESSON FIVE

Objectives
1. To expand upon the idea of being "phony"
2. To give students the chance to stretch their imaginations and have some fun
3. To have students do a different kind of research (rather than the usual encyclopedia work!)
4. To have students focus on a project, research it, study it, and bring it full cycle to completion
5. To get students out of their chairs and actively participating in class
6. To assign the pre-reading activities and the reading of chapters 14-17

Activity #1
Distribute the Character Project Assignment sheet and discuss the directions in detail.

Activity #2
Tell students that prior to the next class period they should have previewed the study questions for, done the vocabulary for and read chapters 14-17. They should begin this reading assignment in class. If you have not yet completed the oral reading evaluations, do so during this class period.

CHARACTER PROJECT ASSIGNMENT - *The Catcher in the Rye*

PROMPT

Holden is always calling everyone a phony. He thinks just about everyone is pretending to be someone they really aren't. In your first writing assignment, you chose a person you would like to be more like (if even for a short while!). Here's a chance for you to be a "phony"--pretend to be someone you aren't.

Your assignment is to choose a person, either your person from Writing Assignment #1 or someone else if you wish, study that person--learn his/her mannerisms, clothing style, speech patterns/accents, everything about him/her you can find and digest--, and create a five minute presentation to perform in front of the class.

HOW TO BEGIN

The first thing is to **choose your person** if you are not using the person you chose in Writing Assignment 1. Return to Writing Assignment #1 for directions on choosing a person if you need help.

Next, **gather information.** Use every resource possible: books, magazines, videos, television episodes, baseball cards--anything that has information that will be useful to you. If you are doing a character from a movie or television show, watch that character over and over again. (Videotape an episode or two if the show is currently running.) If you are doing a character from a book or play, read and reread the book and key parts relating to your character. Keep a little notebook of notes about your person. If your person is a historical figure, look for PBS or cable specials about that person, clips from news shows, books, magazine articles, etc.

PLANNING YOUR PRESENTATION

When you have enough information, begin to plan your presentation.

Character from a Book or Play: Choose your favorite scene from the book and prepare to act it out. Try to have as few characters involved as possible. If others are needed, ask some of your classmates to fill in the parts. You, however, will be responsible for making sure they have the costumes and props they need.

Character from a Television Show or Movie: Choose your favorite scene from the show or movie. Watch it over and over again and prepare to act it out as it is done on film. If other actors are needed, ask some of your classmates to fill in the parts. You, however, are responsible for making sure they have the costumes and props they need.

Historical Figure: Perhaps you would like to be Dr. Martin Luther King, Jr. giving his "I Have a Dream" speech or former President Nixon giving his "I am not a crook..." speech, or Abraham Lincoln delivering the *Gettysburg Address*. Maybe someone like Ben Franklin discovering electricity or Moses getting the Ten Commandments would appeal to you. If you choose a historical figure, you need to create a five minute presentation that would be appropriate for your person.

Catcher in the Rye Character Project Assignment Page 2

Sports Figure: Maybe the person you would like to be is/was an athlete. If so, you need to create a five minute presentation as that person. However, if the person is a basketball player, for example, you may not just spend your five minutes in the gym shooting baskets. You have to find a creative way of showing that person's lifestyle/appeal. If your presentation is videotaped, you may spend a minute or so of your presentation showing your person's mannerisms in his/her sport (on the basketball court, baseball diamond, hockey rink, etc.), but you must include more than just that.

After you have decided upon a scene or created something to present, you need to make a list of **things you will need.** This list should include costumes, props, scripts, etc.--anything you will need to create your presentation. Gather together the things on your list. Make your costumes and props. Practice, practice, practice!

REQUIREMENTS
1. Your presentation must be between five and six minutes long.
2. Your presentation may be made "live" or via videotape.
3. You must play the character you would like to be.
4. You may not use a script, but your supporting actors may if they want to.
5. You will be graded on how well you portray the character, the quality of your research, the physical presentation (loudness, clarity, how well the audience can see and hear you), your enthusiasm for the project, and the amount of time it takes you to set up and clear the performance area (the shorter the time, the better your grade).
6. Your research notes must be handed in on the day your scene is presented.
7. You must be a supporting actor in at least one other person's presentation. You will also be given a grade for your performance as a supporting actor.

LESSON SIX

Objectives
1. To review the main ideas of chapters 14-17
2. To preview the study questions for chapters 18-21
3. To read chapters 18-21
4. To give students the opportunity to use the library to gather information for their character projects

Activity #1
Ask students to get out their books and some paper (not their study guides). Tell students to write down five questions (and answers) which cover the main events and ideas in chapters 8-11.
Discuss the students questions and answers orally, making a list of the questions with brief responses on the board. Put a star next to the students' questions and answers that are essentially the same as the study guide questions. (Be sure that all the study guide questions are answered.)

Activity #2
Take students to the library. Explain to them that this is their chance to use the library to collect any information they can find about their characters. Give students the remainder of this class time to do their library research (or the assignment in Activity #3 if they do not need the library for research).
Remind students that they do have to do the nonfiction reading assignment associated with this unit--to read at least one work of nonfiction and fill out the nonfiction reading assignment sheet. This is a good opportunity to fulfill that requirement.

Activity #3
Tell students to preview the study questions, do the vocabulary work for and read chapters 18-21 prior to your next class period. If students do not need the library resources or if they find sufficient information before the class period is over, they should begin working on this assignment.

LESSON SEVEN

Objectives
    1. To review the main events of chapters 18-21
    2. To check to see that students did the reading assignment
    3. To assign the pre-reading, vocabulary and reading work for chapters 22-26
    4. To give students additional class time to work on their character projects

Activity #1
    Give students a quiz on chapters 18-21. Use either the short answer or multiple choice form of the study guide questions as a quiz so that in discussing the answers to the quiz you also answer the study guide questions. Collect the papers for grade recording.

Activity #2
    Tell students that prior to Lesson Nine (give students a day and a date) they must have completed the pre-reading, vocabulary and reading work for chapters 22-26. Students may have the remainder of this period to work on this assignment.

NOTE: Your students may need some time during this class period to ask other students to be supporting actors in their presentations. It would be a good idea to allow five minutes or so at the end of the period for this purpose.

LESSON EIGHT

Objectives
    1. To review the main ideas and events from chapters 22-26
    2. To discuss *The Catcher in the Rye* on interpretive and critical levels

Activity #1
    Take a few minutes at the beginning of the period to review the study questions for chapters 22-26.

Activity #2
    Choose the questions from the Extra Discussion Questions/Writing Assignments which seem most appropriate for your students. A class discussion of these questions is most effective if students have been given the opportunity to formulate answers to the questions prior to the discussion. To this end, you may either have all the students formulate answers to all the questions, divide your class into groups and assign one or more questions to each group, or you could assign one question to each student in your class. The option you choose will make a difference in the amount of class time needed for this activity.

Activity #3
    After students have had ample time to formulate answers to the questions, begin your class discussion of the questions and the ideas presented by the questions. Be sure students take notes during the discussion so they have information to study for the unit test.

EXTRA WRITING ASSIGNMENTS/DISCUSSION QUESTIONS - *The Catcher in the Rye*

<u>Interpretation</u>

1. Explain how J.D. Salinger's using Holden as the narrator affects our understanding of the events in *The Catcher in the Rye*.

2. If you were to rewrite *The Catcher in the Rye* as a play, where would you start and end each chapter? Explain why.

3. What are the conflicts in the story? Are they resolved by the end of the story? If so, how? If not, why not?

4. What is the setting of the story? How does the setting contribute to ideas presented in the story?

5. Who are the people Holden likes in the story? Why does he like them?

<u>Critical</u>

6. Describe Holden's relationship with Phoebe.

7. Are Holden's actions believably motivated? Explain why or why not.

8. What is the problem with Holden's life?

9. Characterize J.D. Salinger's style of writing. How does it contribute to the value of the novel?

10. Holden often says he is going to call someone, but he doesn't do it because he isn't in the mood. What could these uncompleted calls symbolize?

11. Why can Holden honestly communicate with Phoebe when he cannot with anyone else?

12. What does Holden have against the movies?

13. Explain how the title relates to the events of the novel and the themes of *The Catcher in the Rye*.

14. Compare and contrast Jane Gallagher and Sally Hayes.

15. Compare and contrast Holden's real world with his fantasy world.

16. Are the characters in *The Catcher in the Rye* stereotypes? If so, explain why J.D. Salinger used stereotypes. If not, explain how the characters merit individuality.

The Catcher in the Rye Extra Discussion Questions page 2

17. Why does Holden keep thinking about Jane Gallagher?

18. Why does Holden want to know about the ducks in Central Park?

19. Why did Holden start to cry when Phoebe gave him her Christmas money?

20. What effect did Allie's death have on Holden?

21. Psychoanalyze Holden. What is at the root of his problems?

22. Why can't anyone help Holden?

23. For what was Holden looking during his four-day "vacation"?

24. What kinds of books did Holden like? Why?

25. Discuss the importance and the role of these characters in *The Catcher in the Rye*: Mr. Spencer, Stradlater, Jane Gallagher, Allie, Ernie's mother, Lillian Simmons, Sunny, Sally Hayes, Maurice, the nuns, Carl Luce James Castle, and Mr. Antolini.

26. Explain the symbolic importance of the broken record, the ducks, Grand Central Station, and the hunting hat.

Critical/Personal Response
27. Is Holden a phony?

28. In Chapter 22, Holden asks, "How would you know you weren't being a phony?" Why would Holden think this would be a problem for someone?

29. Was Holden a coward?

30. Do you think the sibling relationship between Holden and Phoebe is realistic? Explain why or why not.

31. Holden thinks most people are a pain in the neck. Is Holden a pain in the neck, too?

32. Is Holden a sympathetic character? (Do we sympathize with him?)

33. Why do you suppose Phoebe decided to go with Holden and not return to school?

The Catcher in the Rye Extra Discussion Questions page 3

34. Is Holden "normal"? Do you think other students at Pencey felt the same way he did?

Personal Response

35. Did you enjoy reading *The Catcher in the Rye*? Why or why not?

36. If Holden had written a poem about his life, what would it have been? Write the poem as you think Holden would have written it.

37. If Holden were a student at your school, would you be his friend? Why or why not?

LESSON NINE

Objective
> To review all of the vocabulary work done in this unit

Activity
> Choose one (or more) of the vocabulary review activities listed below and spend your class period as directed in the activity. Some of the materials for these review activities are located in the Vocabulary Resources section of this unit.

VOCABULARY REVIEW ACTIVITIES

1. Divide your class into two teams and have an old-fashioned spelling or definition bee.

2. Give each of your students (or students in groups of two, three or four) a *The Catcher in the Rye* Vocabulary Word Search Puzzle. The person (group) to find all of the vocabulary words in the puzzle first wins.

3. Give students a *The Catcher in the Rye* Vocabulary Word Search Puzzle without the word list. The person or group to find the most vocabulary words in the puzzle wins.

4. Use a *The Catcher in the Rye* Vocabulary Crossword Puzzle. Put the puzzle onto a transparency on the overhead projector (so everyone can see it), and do the puzzle together as a class.

5. Give students a *The Catcher in the Rye* Vocabulary Matching Worksheet to do.

6. Divide your class into two teams. Use *The Catcher in the Rye* vocabulary words with their letters jumbled as a word list. Student 1 from Team A faces off against Student 1 from Team B. You write the first jumbled word on the board. The first student (1A or 1B) to unscramble the word wins the chance for his/her team to score points. If 1A wins the jumble, go to student 2A and give him/her a definition. He/she must give you the correct spelling of the vocabulary word which fits that definition. If he/she does, Team A scores a point, and you give student 3A a definition for which you expect a correctly spelled matching vocabulary word. Continue giving Team A definitions until some team member makes an incorrect response. An incorrect response sends the game back to the jumbled-word face off, this time with students 2A and 2B. Instead of repeating giving definitions to the first few students of each team, continue with the student after the one who gave the last incorrect response on the team. For example, if Team B wins the jumbled-word face-off, and student 5B gave the last incorrect answer for Team B, you would start this round of definition questions with student 6B, and so on. The team with the most points wins!

7. Have students write a story in which they correctly use as many vocabulary words as possible.

LESSON TEN

<u>Objectives</u>
1. To give students the opportunity to practice writing to inform
2. To have students write introductions and conclusions for their character performances
3. To give the teacher the opportunity to evaluate students' writing
4. To keep the audience from being totally lost while viewing the character performances

<u>Activity</u>
Distribute Writing Assignment #2. Discuss the directions in detail and give students ample time to complete the assignment.

LESSONS ELEVEN AND TWELVE

<u>Objectives</u>
1. To discuss some of the major ideas and themes in the novel
2. To give students a chance to work together in small groups to exchange ideas and find information

<u>Activity#1</u>
Divide your class into six groups--one group for each of the following ideas: religion, education, money, death, people as madmen/crazy, and people are phony.
Allow the groups time to find specific examples of their ideas in the novel. I suggest that the groups assign so-many chapters per person to look for specific examples and write them down. Allow time for the group members to discuss their findings and come up with some intelligent statements about the role of their ideas in the novel. The groups should appoint a spokesperson to report the group's thoughts.

<u>Activity #2</u>
Call on individual group members by chapter(s) to give the examples they found of their topic in those chapters. Jot them down briefly for students to copy into their notes.
Ask the group's spokesperson to give the group's thoughts about the topic's development so far. Jot these down. Ask if anyone from the group has anything to add. Take the time to discuss each topic thoroughly with the class and be sure to allow time for students to express their ideas or ask questions.

WRITING ASSIGNMENT #2 - *The Catcher in the Rye*

PROMPT

By now you should know what character you are going to portray and what material you will be presenting for your character project. So that your audience isn't totally confused, you need to tell us who you are, and what material you are presenting. You need to set the scene for us--tell us what has gone on before the scene you are going to do. Likewise, after your presentation is concluded, and we're all interested in your character, you have to tell us what happens to your character after your scene.

If your character is an historical figure or an athlete, you should tell us a little bit about his/her life prior to the age he/she is during your presentation, and likewise, what happened to him/her after the age he/she is during your presentation.

Your assignment is to write a short composition in which you introduce your character, tell about the time prior to your presentation, and tell about the time after your presentation.

PREWRITING

First, jot down your character's name, and a few remarks which will adequately identify him/her for your audience.

Next, make a few notes about things that are important for your audience to know about your character prior to the time you are portraying in your presentation.

Finally, make a few notes about things that the audience will probably want to know about what happens to your character after the time you are portraying in your presentation.

DRAFTING

First write an introductory paragraph in which you introduce your character.
Next write one paragraph in which you give the background information.
Then write one paragraph in which you give the post-presentation information.

PROMPT

When you finish the rough draft of your paper, ask a student who sits near you to read it. After reading your rough draft, he/she should tell you what he/she liked best about your work, which parts were difficult to understand, and ways in which your work could be improved. Reread your paper considering your critic's comments, and make the corrections you think are necessary.

PROOFREADING

Do a final proofreading of your paper double-checking your grammar, spelling, organization, and the clarity of your ideas.

LESSONS THIRTEEN AND FOURTEEN

Objective
    To complete the character projects for this unit

Activity
    Have students do their character presentations for the class. Students should use their Writing Assignment #2s to give the appropriate introduction, do the presentation, and then use Writing Assignment #2s to give the post-presentation information.

Note: Make sure you have a video player and television ready for those students who videotaped their presentations.

LESSON FIFTEEN

Objectives
    1. To give students the opportunity to practice writing to persuade
    2. To review the main events and ideas in the book
    3. To give the teacher the opportunity to evaluate students' writing skills

Activity #1
    Distribute Writing Assignment #3. Discuss the directions in detail and give students ample time to complete the assignment.

Activity #2
    While students are working on Writing Assignment #3, call individual students to your desk or some other private area for writing conferences regarding the first two writing assignments in this unit. An evaluation form is included with this unit for your convenience to help you structure your conference.
    After you have had your conference, tell each student that he/she must rewrite the composition(s) taking into consideration your suggestions. Tell students when the revisions will be due.
    I suggest grading the revisions on an A-C-E scale (A=all revisions done correctly, C=some revisions done correctly, E=revisions not attempted or done very poorly). This will give each student credit for his/her work, but will greatly speed up your grading time.

LESSON SIXTEEN

Objective
    To review the main ideas presented in *The Catcher in the Rye*

Activity
    Choose one of the review games/activities included in the packet and spend your class period as outlined there. Some materials for these activities are located in the Unit Resource section of this unit.

WRITING EVALUATION FORM - *The Catcher in the Rye*

Name _____ Date _____

      Grade _____

Circle One For Each Item:

Grammar: correct errors noted on paper

Spelling: correct errors noted on paper

Punctuation: correct errors noted on paper

Legibility: excellent   good   fair   poor

Strengths:

Weaknesses:

Comments/Suggestions:

WRITING ASSIGNMENT #3 - *The Catcher in the Rye*

PROMPT
You are a student at Holden's school, and you're sick and tired of hearing him calling everyone a phony. You meet him after school one day and persuade him that everyone is NOT a phony. Your assignment is to write a composition telling what you would say to Holden to convince him that everyone is not a phony.

PREWRITING
Put on your thinking cap. How in the world are you going to convince Holden that everyone is not a phony? Start with the root of the problem: Why does he call everyone a phony? Jot down your answer to that question on a piece of paper. Next to that, write down three good reasons/ways of how you can overcome the root of the problem. Next to each of the reasons, give examples or ideas that support your statements.

DRAFTING
Write your paper as if you were talking to Holden. Start with an introductory paragraph in which you bring up the subject that he's always calling people phonies.

In the body of your composition, write one paragraph for each of the reasons/ways you jotted down for overcoming the root of the problem. Use a topic sentence for each of your three paragraphs, and fill in the paragraphs with the examples or ideas that support your statements.

Write a concluding paragraph in which you end your (rather one-sided) conversation with Holden.

PROMPT
When you finish the rough draft of your paper, ask a student who sits near you to read it. After reading your rough draft, he/she should tell you what he/she liked best about your work, which parts were difficult to understand, and ways in which your work could be improved. Reread your paper considering your critic's comments, and make the corrections you think are necessary.

PROOFREADING
Do a final proofreading of your paper double-checking your grammar, spelling, organization, and the clarity of your ideas.

REVIEW GAMES/ACTIVITIES - *The Catcher in the Rye*

1. Ask the class to make up a unit test for *The Catcher in the Rye*. The test should have 4 sections: matching, true/false, short answer, and essay. Students may use 1/2 period to make the test and then swap papers and use the other 1/2 class period to take a test a classmate has devised. (open book) You may want to use the unit test included in this packet or take questions from the students' unit tests to formulate your own test.

2. Take 1/2 period for students to make up true and false questions (including the answers). Collect the papers and divide the class into two teams. Draw a big tic-tac-toe board on the chalk board. Make one team X and one team O. Ask questions to each side, giving each student one turn. If the question is answered correctly, that student's team's letter (X or O) is placed in the box. If the answer is incorrect, no mark is placed in the box. The object is to get three marks in a row like tic-tac-toe. You may want to keep track of the number of games won for each team.

3. Take 1/2 period for students to make up questions (true/false and short answer). Collect the questions. Divide the class into two teams. You'll alternate asking questions to individual members of teams A & B (like in a spelling bee). The question keeps going from A to B until it is correctly answered, then a new question is asked. A correct answer does not allow the team to get another question. Correct answers are +2 points; incorrect answers are -1 point.

4. Have students pair up and quiz each other from their study guides and class notes.

5. Give students a *The Catcher in the Rye* crossword puzzle to complete.

6. Divide your class into two teams. Use *The Catcher in the Rye* crossword words with their letters jumbled as a word list. Student 1 from Team A faces off against Student 1 from Team B. You write the first jumbled word on the board. The first student (1A or 1B) to unscramble the word wins the chance for his/her team to score points. If 1A wins the jumble, go to student 2A and give him/her a clue. He/she must give you the correct word which matches that clue. If he/she does, Team A scores a point, and you give student 3A a clue for which you expect another correct response. Continue giving Team A clues until some team member makes an incorrect response. An incorrect response sends the game back to the jumbled-word face off, this time with students 2A and 2B. Instead of repeating giving clues to the first few students of each team, continue with the student after the one who gave the last incorrect response on the team. For example, if Team B wins the jumbled-word face-off, and student 5B gave the last incorrect answer for Team B, you would start this round of clue questions with student 6B, and so on. The team with the most points wins!

UNIT TESTS

SHORT ANSWER UNIT TEST 1 - *The Catcher in the Rye*

I. Matching/Identify

___ 1. Phoebe   A. Student at Whooton; has a drink with Holden

___ 2. Antolini   B. Holden's theater date

___ 3. Ackley   C. Holden's dead brother

___ 4. Sally   D. English teacher

___ 5. D. B.   E. Holden's history teacher

___ 6. Luce   F. Committed suicide

___ 7. Spencer   G. Holden's sister

___ 8. Allie   H. Roomed next to Holden at Pencey

___ 9. Stradlater   I. Holden's former girl friend

___ 10. James Castle   J. Holden's roommate at Pencey

___ 11. Jane Gallagher   K. Holden's brother in Hollywood

___ 12. Lillian Simmons   L. DB's old girlfriend

II. Short Answer

1. Where is Holden as he narrates the story?

2. Why wouldn't Holden be back to Pencey after Christmas vacation?

3. Where did Holden decide to go? Why?

The Catcher in the Rye Short Answer Unit Test 1 Page 2

4. Describe Holden's relationship with Jane Gallagher.

5. What was the "big mess" Holden got into when he got back to the hotel after being at Ernie's?

6. What made Holden "not so depressed anymore" on his way to the record store?

7. Why didn't Holden like actors?

8. Why did Holden like the museum so much?

9. Why did Holden go to Mr. Antolini's house?

10. Why did Holden sit on the bench in the rain even though it was coming down in buckets?

The Catcher in the Rye Short Answer Unit Test 1 Page 3

III. Composition

What is the point of *Catcher in the Rye*? When we read books, we usually come away from our reading experience a little richer, having given more thought to a particular aspect of life. What do you think J. D. Salinger intended us to gain from reading his novel?

The Catcher in the Rye Short Answer Unit Test 1 Page 4

IV. Vocabulary
    Listen to the vocabulary words and write them down.
    Go back later and fill in the correct definition for each word.

1.

2.

3.

4.

5.

6.

7.

8.

9.

10.

SHORT ANSWER UNIT TEST 2 - *The Catcher in the Rye*

I. Matching/Identify

___ 1. Phoebe   A. Roomed next to Holden at Pencey

___ 2. Antolini   B. Holden's history teacher

___ 3. Ackley   C. Holden's sister

___ 4. Sally   D. English teacher

___ 5. D. B.   E. Holden's roommate at Pencey

___ 6. Luce   F. DB's old girlfriend

___ 7. Spencer   G. Holden's brother in Hollywood

___ 8. Allie   H. Student at Whooton; has a drink with Holden

___ 9. Stradlater   I. Holden's former girl friend

___ 10. James Castle   J. Holden's theater date

___ 11. Jane Gallagher K. Holden's dead brother

___ 12. Lillian Simmons L. Committed suicide

II. Short Answer

1. What "dirty trick" did Mr. Spencer pull on Holden?

2. Where did Holden decide to go when he left Pencey early? Why?

3. Why did Holden lie to Ernie's mother on the train?

The Catcher in the Rye Short Answer Unit Test 2 Page 2

4. Holden said he felt like committing suicide. Why didn't he?

5. Who did Holden meet at the "little sandwich bar" after he locked his bags at the station? What did they talk about?

6. Why did Holden like the museum so much?

7. How did Holden's feelings for Sally change from the beginning of the date to the end?

8. What was Holden's reply when Phoebe asked him why he "got the ax again"?

9. What advice did Mr. Antolini give Holden?

10. How did Holden explain his catcher in the rye daydream?

The Catcher in the Rye Short Answer Unit Test 2 Page 3

III. Composition

    Choose one word that best describes Holden and write a composition in which you explain why you chose that word. Use specific examples from the text to support your ideas, and show as much knowledge of the book as you can.

The Catcher in the Rye Short Answer Unit Test 2 Page 4

IV. Vocabulary

    Listen to the vocabulary words and write them down.
    Go back later and write in the correct definitions.

1.

2.

3.

4.

5.

6.

7.

8.

9.

10.

KEY: SHORT ANSWER UNIT TESTS - *The Catcher in the Rye*

The short answer questions are taken directly from the study guides.
If you need to look up the answers, you will find them in the study guide section.

Answers to the composition questions will vary depending on your
class discussions and the level of your students.

For the vocabulary section of the test, choose ten of the
words from the vocabulary lists to read orally for your students.

The answers to the matching section of the test are below.

Answers to the matching section of the Advanced Short Answer Unit Test
are the same as for Short Answer Unit Test #2.

<u>Test #1</u>
1. G
2. D
3. H
4. B
5. K
6. A
7. E
8. C
9. J
10. F
11. I
12. L

<u>Test #2</u>
1. C
2. D
3. A
4. J
5. G
6. H
7. B
8. K
9. E
10. L
11. I
12. F

ADVANCED SHORT ANSWER UNIT TEST - *The Catcher in the Rye*

I. Matching/Identify

___ 1. Phoebe   A. Roomed next to Holden at Pencey

___ 2. Antolini   B. Holden's history teacher

___ 3. Ackley   C. Holden's sister

___ 4. Sally   D. English teacher

___ 5. D. B.   E. Holden's roommate at Pencey

___ 6. Luce   F. DB's old girlfriend

___ 7. Spencer   G. Holden's brother in Hollywood

___ 8. Allie   H. Student at Whooton; has a drink with Holden

___ 9. Stradlater   I. Holden's former girl friend

___ 10. James Castle   J. Holden's theater date

___ 11. Jane Gallagher   K. Holden's dead brother

___ 12. Lillian Simmons   L. Committed suicide

II. Short Answer

1. Explain the symbolic significance of:
    a. the broken record

    b. the ducks

    c. Grand Central Station

Catcher in the Rye Advanced Short Answer Unit Test Page 2

2. Compare and contrast Jane Gallagher and Sally Hayes.

3. Why can Holden honestly communicate with Phoebe even though he cannot with anyone else?

4. Compare and contrast Holden's real world with his fantasy world.

5. What effect did Allie's death have on Holden?

6. Discuss the idea of religion in the book *The Catcher in the Rye*.

7. Discuss the idea of people as madmen/crazy in the book *The Catcher in the Rye*.

8. Explain the significance of the title of *The Catcher in the Rye*.

Catcher in the Rye Advanced Short Answer Unit Test Page 3

III. Composition

"Don't ever tell anybody anything. If you do, you start missing everybody."
Explain these last two lines of the book in relation to the events and ideas in the book, *The Catcher in the Rye*.

Catcher in the Rye Advanced Short Answer Unit Test Page 4

IV. Vocabulary

Listen to the vocabulary words and write them down. Go back later and use all of the words in a composition. The composition must in some way relate to *The Catcher in the Rye*.

MULTIPLE CHOICE UNIT TEST 1 - *The Catcher in the Rye*

I. Matching/Identify

___ 1. Phoebe   A. Student at Whooton; has a drink with Holden

___ 2. Antolini   B. Holden's theater date

___ 3. Ackley   C. Holden's dead brother

___ 4. Sally   D. English teacher

___ 5. D. B.   E. Holden's history teacher

___ 6. Luce   F. Committed suicide

___ 7. Spencer   G. Holden's sister

___ 8. Allie   H. Roomed next to Holden at Pencey

___ 9. Stradlater   I. Holden's former girl friend

___ 10. James Castle   J. Holden's roommate at Pencey

___ 11. Jane Gallagher   K. Holden's brother in Hollywood

___ 12. Lillian Simmons   L. DB's old girlfriend

Catcher in the Rye Multiple Choice Unit Test 1 Page 2

II. Multiple Choice

1. Why wouldn't Holden be back to Pencey after Christmas vacation?
    a. He had been expelled because he failed four of five subjects.
    b. He had lost his athletic scholarship and could not afford the tuition.
    c. He had been given an early acceptance to college and was starting the next semester.
    d. His father was sick and he had to go to work to help support the family.

2. What "dirty trick" did Mr. Spencer pull on Holden?
    a. He orally read back Holden's exam answer and the note Holden had written.
    b. He had a surprise going away party, even though Holden had said he didn't want a party.
    c. He pretended to be dead to scare Holden.
    d. He called Holden's parents while Holden was present and discussed his (Holden's) situation with them.

3. Whom did Holden meet on his train ride? Why did he lie to her?
    a. He met a friend of his mother's. He lied because he was afraid she would tell his mother she saw him.
    b. He met the mother of a school mate. He lied because he wanted the mother to feel proud of her son, and he wanted to tell her what she wanted to hear.
    c. He met a friend who had graduated from Pencey the previous year. He lied because he was embarrassed to admit that he had flunked out.
    e. He met one of his teachers from elementary school He lied because she had always had a good opinion of him, and he didn't want to change that.

4. Describe Holden's relationship with Jane Gallagher.
    a. They have been romantically involved for over a year, although they are currently having a disagreement because Jane wants to date others and Holden doesn't.
    b. They seem to be good friends, playing checkers, going to movies, and talking. There was no advanced romantic involvement between them.
    c. They used to be romantically involved but now they can't stand each other.
    d. They have only spoken a few times, but Holden would like to get to know her better.

5. What do we learn about Holden from his diversion about his gloves being stolen at Pencey?
    a. He calls himself a coward, but he is really too humane to hurt anyone.
    b. He is very selfish and materialistic.
    c. He will jump at any chance to fight.
    d. Possessions don't mean a lot to him.

Catcher in the Rye Multiple Choice Unit Test 1 Page 3

6. Holden said he felt like committing suicide. Why didn't he do it?
    a. He wanted to write a letter to Phoebe first, but he didn't have paper or pencil, so he decided to wait.
    b. He was afraid he might not succeed, and then he would have to face his parents.
    c. He didn't want a bunch of "stupid rubbernecks" looking at him all gory.
    d. He was going to jump out the window, but he couldn't get it open. He got tired of trying, and fell asleep.

7. Whom did Holden meet at the sandwich bar? What did they talk about?
    a. He met Sunny. They talked about what had happened the night before.
    b. He met two nuns. They talked about literature and Holden's views on *Romeo and Juliet.*
    c. He met Stradlater. They talked about school and Holden's personal problems.
    d. He met Ernie, the piano player. They talked about Holden's brother.

8. What record did Holden get for Phoebe? Why?
    a. He got "Little Shirley Beans." He liked it and though Phoebe would, too.
    b. He got "The Skaters' Waltz" by Strauss because it was her favorite skating song.
    c. He got Shirley Temple singing, "On the Good Ship Lollipop." Phoebe liked to pretend she was Shirley Temple.
    d. He got "The Twelve Days of Christmas," because he knew she had to learn it for the school play.

9. What made Holden "not so depressed anymore" on his way to the record store?
    a. He was energized by the lights and all of the activity on Broadway.
    b. He watched some jugglers and street mimes and they made him laugh.
    c. He hears a young boy singing, "If a body catch a body coming through the rye."
    d. He started praying and realized that praying helped him a lot.

10. What did Holden like best about the museum?
    a. It was free on Sundays.
    b. Everything always stayed where it was.
    c. It reminded him of fun times with his parents and brothers when he was young.
    d. It was warm and cheerful, and no one bothered him.

Catcher in the Rye Multiple Choice Unit Test 1 Page 4

11. Describe Holden's feelings for Sally at the beginning of the date and at the end.
    a. He started out by saying he loved her and they talked of marriage. By the end of the date he hated her.
    b. He didn't like her much at the beginning, but by the end he was in love and proposed to her.
    c. He liked her somewhat at the beginning, by the time the date was over he was in love.
    d. He didn't like her at first, and really hated her by the end.

12. Why did Holden call Carl Luce even though he didn't like him much?
    a. Holden was desperate for companionship, and also though Luce was intellectual and could help him.
    b. He wanted to borrow money. He knew Luce was rich, and was a sucker for a sob story.
    c. Luce has his own apartment. Holden wants Luce to let him stay with him until Wednesday, when he can go home.
    d. Holden knew Luce was an A student. He wanted Luce to tutor him over the holidays.

13. What was Holden's reply when Phoebe asked him why he "got the ax again"?
    a. He said the work was too hard because he had not been adequately prepared at the last school.
    b. He said it was unfair, that the teachers just didn't like him and were out to get him.
    c. He said it was because the president of the school board and his (Holden's) father had a political disagreement. Holden was being expelled to get even with his father.
    d. He said it was one of the worst school he ever attended, full of phonies and mean guys.

14. What advice did Mr. Antolini give Holden?
    a. "Only educated and scholarly men are able to contribute something valuable to this world."
    b. "I simply find Eastern philosophy more interesting than Western."
    c. "The mark of the immature man is that he wants to die only for a cause, while the mark of a mature man is that he wants to live humbly for one."
    d. "You're a real prince; a gentleman and a scholar."

15. Why did Holden sit on the bench in the rain even though it was coming down in buckets?
    a. He was enjoying watching Phoebe ride the carousel.
    b. He wanted to get sick enough to have to go into the hospital for a while.
    c. He was drunk and didn't realize what he was doing.
    d. He was punishing himself for behaving so badly.

Catcher in the Rye Multiple Choice Unit Test 1 Page 5

16. How did Holden explain his catcher in the rye daydream?
    a. He would be running through a field of rye and farmers with pitchforks would be chasing him.
    b. He would play baseball wearing his brother's glove, and stand in the outfield, ready to catch anything that came his way.
    c. He would stand guard over all of the rye whiskey in the world and make sure no one got drunk.
    d. He would stand in a field of rye, where his job would be to catch any children who started to go over the cliff.

III. Composition

Why is Holden in the rest home in California? Does he belong there? Explain your answer thoroughly.

Catcher in the Rye Multiple Choice Unit Test 1 Page 6

IV. Vocabulary

___ 1. Fascinated   a. Attentive to duty; diligent

___ 2. Groping   b. Meaning opposite of what is expressed

___ 3. Inferiority   c. Drive out by force

___ 4. Pacifist   d. Privately; personally; very closely

___ 5. Conscientious   e. Mutual; equivalent; interchangeable

___ 6. Pedagogical   f. A person skilled in taking shorthand

___ 7. Ironical   g. Held the attention of; captivated

___ 8. Louse   h. Of an upper class; distinguished

___ 9. Halitosis   i. Feelings of doubt

___10. Stenographer   j. A person regarded as mean or contemptible

___11. Frock   k. Bad smelling breath

___12. Intimately   l. One who opposed the use of force under any circumstances

___13. Expel   m. Noisy; unruly

___14. Humble   n. Characteristic of teaching or teachers

___15. Boisterous   o. Lowly; unpretentious

___16. Unanimous   p. Often

___17. Frequently   q. Showing or based on total agreement

___18. Reciprocal   r. Reaching blindly

___19. Qualms   s. Strong feelings of inadequacy

___20. Aristocratic   t. Coat; cloak

MULTIPLE CHOICE UNIT TEST 2 - *The Catcher in the Rye*

I. Matching

___ 1. Phoebe   A. Roomed next to Holden at Pencey

___ 2. Antolini   B. Holden's history teacher

___ 3. Ackley   C. Holden's sister

___ 4. Sally   D. English teacher

___ 5. D. B.   E. Holden's roommate at Pencey

___ 6. Luce   F. DB's old girlfriend

___ 7. Spencer   G. Holden's brother in Hollywood

___ 8. Allie   H. Student at Whooton; has a drink with Holden

___ 9. Stradlater   I. Holden's former girl friend

___ 10. James Castle   J. Holden's theater date

___ 11. Jane Gallagher   K. Holden's dead brother

___ 12. Lillian Simmons   L. Committed suicide

Catcher in the Rye Multiple Choice Unit Test 2 Page 2

II. Multiple Choice

1. Why wouldn't Holden be back to Pencey after Christmas vacation?
    a. He had lost his athletic scholarship and could not afford the tuition.
    b. He had been expelled because he failed four of five subjects.
    c. He had been given an early acceptance to college and was starting the next semester.
    d. His father was sick and he had to go to work to help support the family.

2. What "dirty trick" did Mr. Spencer pull on Holden?
    a. He pretended to be dead to scare Holden.
    b. He had a surprise going away party, even though Holden had said he didn't want a party.
    c. He orally rad back Holden's exam answer and the note Holden had written.
    d. He called Holden's parents while Holden was present and discussed his (Holden's) situation with them.

3. Whom did Holden meet on his train ride? Why did he lie to her?
    a. He met a friend of his mother's. He lied because he was afraid she would tell his mother she saw him.
    b. He met one of his teachers from elementary school. He lied because she had always had a good opinion of him, and he didn't want to change that.
    c. He met a friend who had graduated from Pencey the previous year. He lied because he was embarrassed to admit that he had flunked out.
    d. He met the mother of a school mate. He lied because he wanted the mother to feel proud of her son, and he wanted to tell her what she wanted to hear.

4. Describe Holden's relationship with Jane Gallagher.
    a. They have been romantically involved for over a year, although they are currently having a disagreement because Jane wants to date others and Holden doesn't.
    b. They used to be romantically involved but now they can't stand each other.
    c. They seem to be good friends, playing checkers, going to movies, and talking. There was no advanced romantic involvement between them.
    d. They have only spoken a few times, but Holden would like to get to know her better.

5. What do we learn about Holden from his diversion about his gloves being stolen at Pencey?
    a. Possessions don't mean a lot to him.
    b. He is very selfish and materialistic.
    c. He will jump at any chance to fight.
    d. He calls himself a coward, but he is really too humane to hurt anyone.

Catcher in the Rye Multiple Choice Unit Test 2 Page 3

6. Holden said he felt like committing suicide. Why didn't he do it?
    a. He didn't want a bunch of "stupid rubbernecks" looking at him all gory.
    b. He was afraid he might not succeed, and then he would have to face his parents.
    c. He wanted to write a letter to Phoebe first, but he didn't have paper or pencil, so he decided to wait.
    d. He was going to jump out the window, but he couldn't get it open. He got tired of trying, and fell asleep.

7. Whom did Holden meet at the sandwich bar? What did they talk about?
    a. He met Sunny. They talked about what had happened the night before.
    b. He met Stradlater. They talked about school and Holden's personal problems.
    c. He met two nuns. They talked about literature and Holden's views on *Romeo and Juliet.*
    d. He met Ernie, the piano player. They talked about Holden's brother.

8. What record did Holden get for Phoebe? Why?
    a. He got "The Skaters' Waltz" by Strauss because it was her favorite skating song.
    b. He got "Little Shirley Beans." He liked it and though Phoebe would, too.
    c. He got Shirley Temple singing, "On the Good Ship Lollipop." Phoebe liked to pretend she was Shirley Temple.
    d. He got "The Twelve Days of Christmas," because he knew she had to learn it for the school play.

9. What made Holden "not so depressed anymore" on his way to the record store?
    a. He was energized by the lights and all of the activity on Broadway.
    b. He watched some jugglers and street mimes and they made him laugh.
    c. He started praying and realized that praying helped him a lot.
    d. He hears a young boy singing, "If a body catch a body coming through the rye."

10. What did Holden like best about the museum?
    a. Everything always stayed where it was.
    b. It was free on Sundays.
    c. It reminded him of fun times with his parents and brothers when he was young.
    d. It was warm and cheerful, and no one bothered him.

Catcher in the Rye Multiple Choice Unit Test 2 Page 4

11. Describe Holden's feelings for Sally at the beginning of the date and at the end.
    a. He didn't like her much at the beginning, but by the end he was in love and proposed to her.
    b. He started out by saying he loved her and they talked of marriage. By the end of the date he hated her.
    c. He liked her somewhat at the beginning, by the time the date was over he was in love.
    d. He didn't like her at first, and really hated her by the end.

12. Why did Holden call Carl Luce even though he didn't like him much?
    a. Holden knew Luce was an A student. He wanted Luce to tutor him over the holidays.
    b. He wanted to borrow money. He knew Luce was rich, and was a sucker for a sob story.
    c. Luce has his own apartment. Holden wants Luce to let him stay with him until Wednesday, when he can go home.
    d. Holden was desperate for companionship, and also thought Luce was intellectual and could help him.

13. What was Holden's reply when Phoebe asked him why he "got the ax again"?
    a. He said the work was too hard because he had not been adequately prepared at the last school.
    b. He said it was one of the worst school he ever attended, full of phonies and mean guys.
    c. He said it was because the president of the school board and his (Holden's) father had a political disagreement. Holden was being expelled to get even with his father.
    d. He said it was unfair, that the teachers just didn't like him and were out to get him.

14. What advice did Mr. Antolini give Holden?
    a. "Only educated and scholarly men are able to contribute something valuable to this world."
    b. "I simply find Eastern philosophy more interesting than Western."
    c. "You're a real prince; a gentleman and a scholar."
    d. "The mark of the immature man is that he wants to die only for a cause, while the mark of a mature man is that he wants to live humbly for one."

15. Why did Holden sit on the bench in the rain even though it was coming down in buckets?
    a. He wanted to get sick enough to have to go into the hospital for a while.
    b. He was enjoying watching Phoebe ride the carousel.
    c. He was drunk and didn't realize what he was doing.
    d. He was punishing himself for behaving so badly.

Catcher in the Rye Multiple Choice Unit Test 2 Page 5

16. How did Holden explain his catcher in the rye daydream?
 a. He would stand in a field of rye, where his job would be to catch any children who started to go over the cliff.
 b. He would play baseball wearing his brother's glove, and stand in the outfield, ready to catch anything that came his way.
 c. He would stand guard over all of the rye whiskey in the world and make sure no one got drunk.
 d. He would be running through a field of rye and farmers with pitchforks would be chasing him.

III. Composition
 One might say Holden walks to the tune of a different drummer; he is a bit out of step with the rest of the world. His attitudes and actions don't fit what the majority of people in our world do. Write a composition in which you defend that statement using specific examples from the novel.

Catcher in the Rye Multiple Choice Unit Test 2 Page 6

IV. Vocabulary

___ 1. Compulsory   a. Mutual; equivalent; interchangeable

___ 2. Lavish   b. One who opposed the use of force under any circumstances

___ 3. Sophisticated   c. Showing or based on total agreement

___ 4. Humble   d. Meaning opposite of what is expressed

___ 5. Pedagogical   e. Grating

___ 6. Raspy   f. Smug; conventional; materialistic

___ 7. Reciprocal   g. Generous or liberal in giving or spending

___ 8. Stenographer   h. Strong feelings of inadequacy

___ 9. Intimately   i. Characteristic of teaching or teachers

___10. Capacity   j. Worldly wise; refined

___11. Qualms   k. Ability to contain, absorb, receive and hold

___12. Bourgeois   l. A person who believes there is no god

___13. Unanimous   m. A person skilled in taking shorthand

___14. Ironical   n. Feelings of doubt

___15. Ostracized   o. Required; must be done

___16. Frequently   p. Lowly; unpretentious

___17. Atheist   q. Privately; personally; very closely

___18. Pacifist   r. Having done something so much as to be bored by it

___19. Blase   s. Shunned; excluded; left out

___20. Inferiority   t. Often

ANSWER SHEET - *The Catcher in the Rye*
Multiple Choice Unit Tests

I. Matching	II. Multiple Choice	IV. Vocabulary
1. ___	1. ___	1. ___
2. ___	2. ___	2. ___
3. ___	3. ___	3. ___
4. ___	4. ___	4. ___
5. ___	5. ___	5. ___
6. ___	6. ___	6. ___
7. ___	7. ___	7. ___
8. ___	8. ___	8. ___
9. ___	9. ___	9. ___
10. ___	10. ___	10. ___
11. ___	11. ___	11. ___
12. ___	12. ___	12. ___
	13. ___	13. ___
	14. ___	14. ___
	15. ___	15. ___
	16. ___	16. ___
		17. ___
		18. ___
		19. ___
		20. ___

ANSWER KEY MULTIPLE CHOICE UNIT TESTS – *Catcher in the Rye*

Answers to Unit Test 1 are in the left column. Answers to Unit Test 2 are in the right column.

I. Matching		II. Multiple Choice		IV. Vocabulary	
1. G	C	1. A	A	1. G	O
2. D	D	2. A	C	2. R	G
3. H	A	3. B	D	3. S	J
4. B	J	4. B	C	4. L	P
5. K	G	5. A	D	5. A	I
6. A	H	6. C	A	6. N	E
7. E	B	7. B	C	7. B	A
8. C	K	8. A	B	8. J	M
9. J	E	9. C	D	9. K	Q
10. F	L	10. B	A	10. F	K
11. I	I	11. A	B	11. T	N
12. L	F	12. A	D	12. D	F
		13. D	B	13. C	C
		14. C	D	14. O	D
		15. A	B	15. M	S
		16. D	A	16. Q	T
				17. P	L
				18. E	B
				19. I	R
				20. H	H

UNIT RESOURCE MATERIALS

BULLETIN BOARD IDEAS - *The Catcher in the Rye*

1. Save one corner of the board for the best of students' *The Catcher in the Rye* writing assignments.

2. Take one of the word search puzzles from the extra activities packet and with a marker copy it over in a large size on the bulletin board. Write the clue words to find to one side. Invite students prior to and after class to find the words and circle them on the bulletin board.

3. Write several of the most significant quotations from the book onto the board on brightly colored paper.

4. Make a bulletin board listing the vocabulary words for this unit. As you complete sections of the novel and discuss the vocabulary for each section, write the definitions on the bulletin board. (If your board is one students face frequently, it will help them learn the words.)

5. Have each student bring in a picture of something that is "phony" -- anything that can be tacked up onto the bulletin board.

6. Title the board: THE CATCHER IN THE RYE. Find pictures of things that are related to the book: a duck, Central Park, a red cap, a carousel, Broadway, a hotel elevator, a movie marquee, a baseball glove, a field of rye, a lawyer, an actor, a museum, a suitcase, Grand Central Station, a school, a prostitute, etc. Post them randomly on the board, showing Holden's random acceptance of all data, his lack of ability to sort things out.

7. Make a bulletin board about New York City, showing pictures of the usual tourist sights, giving information about plays currently running on Broadway, etc.

8. Have students bring in pictures of their people for the character project, and post these on the board.

9. Check your library for a detailed biography of J.D. Salinger, and write that up on the bulletin board for students to read in their spare time. Articles of criticism about *Catcher* would also be appropriate on this board.

10. Make a bulletin board with hotlines for troubled youths to call.

EXTRA ACTIVITIES

One of the difficulties in teaching a novel is that all students don't read at the same speed. One student who likes to read may take the book home and finish it in a day or two. Sometimes a few students finish the in-class assignments early. The problem, then, is finding suitable extra activities for students.

The best thing I've found is to keep a little library in the classroom. For this unit on *The Catcher in the Rye,* you might check out from the school library other related books like *Out of Africa, The Return of the Native, Of Human Bondage, The Great Gatsby, A Farewell to Arms, Romeo and Juliet* (books Holden mentions), or stories by Ring Lardner. Books or articles about skating, movies, city life, depression, private schools, New York, Grand Central Station, or Broadway would be good, too.

Other things you may keep on hand are puzzles. We have made some relating directly to *The Catcher in the Rye* for you. Feel free to duplicate them.

Some students may like to draw. You might devise a contest or allow some extra-credit grade for students who draw characters or scenes from *The Catcher in the Rye*. Note, too, that if the students do not want to keep their drawings you may pick up some extra bulletin board materials this way. If you have a contest and you supply the prize (a CD or something like that perhaps), you could, possibly, make the drawing itself a non-refundable entry fee.

The pages which follow contain games, puzzles and worksheets. The keys, when appropriate, immediately follow the puzzle or worksheet. There are two main groups of activities: one group for the unit; that is, generally relating to *The Catcher in the Rye* text, and another group of activities related strictly to *The Catcher in the Rye* vocabulary.

Directions for these games, puzzles and worksheets are self-explanatory. The object here is to provide you with extra materials you may use in any way you choose.

MORE ACTIVITIES - *The Catcher in the Rye*

1. Pick a chapter or scene with a great deal of dialogue and have the students act it out on a stage. (Perhaps you could assign various scenes to different groups of students so more than one scene could be acted and more students could participate.)

2. If you have a class of good readers, you might tell students that they each have to read one of the books Holden mentions in *Catcher*. Have them give an oral report telling about the book explaining how the book relates to the ideas presented in *Catcher*.

3. Take a day or two to study the history and attractions of New York City. If you live close enough, perhaps take a field trip to see Broadway, Radio City Music Hall, and other places mentioned in the book.

4. Have students design a book cover (front and back and inside flaps) for *The Catcher in the Rye*.

5. Have students design a bulletin board (ready to be put up; not just sketched) for *The Catcher in the Rye*.

6. Discuss Holden's language; why he talks the way he does.

7. Discuss what Holden's options were when he was failing in school. What kinds of things could Holden have done to have saved himself from having a breakdown? What kinds of options are available for students today?

8. Discuss Holden's four days as a mini-epic journey.

9. Have students make a board game using the places, events and ideas from the novel.

10. Sometimes, like Holden, people would like to express themselves to a friend, relative, or teacher, but they simply don't know how to do it without feeling embarrassed or awkward. Discuss or role-play some ways to approach this problem.

WORD SEARCH - *The Catcher in the Rye*

All words in this list are associated with *The Catcher in the Rye*. The words are placed backwards, forward, diagonally, up and down. The included words are listed below the word searches.

```
Z S M Z R P J K R M W M N X R E Z N Y E Y V S T
E F G U S W R G M S E R K F R V N N C L I W V Z
W S Q A S L B E Z L A Y E N K I L U L N R L K T
P H O E B E R U T A M M I G A L L A G H E R L X
X R B N A E U S Z A A E T R N C S E V L W E J A
L G R N H M A M D U L T T S M I T F S E O K R H
G Y S C Y C J T R H K D N T I O L O A U N V D G
R Z T N S A B I N U N S A R L R R A R I O D E H
D A N K X D C X P B C N E R A H H O S S L R E L
C U Z S S E K K K M T C B D T R Z C N M N E A R
S D M M P J C S L O N G I X B S Z X K P T L D C
Z F E N C I N G L E P O C A U L F I E L D R L F
F O P J W O M I P X Y Y V L Q W W K Z Q B J L R
P H D W M K N S H F G Q W R R B S S G C V F T B
F M N M T I Y R J X M M M L K M B Q K L S Q G T
V S I M D B M G B L J W M M B V Q S Q Y R G Z W
N S Z N R P F W Q V P S B R L S W S F Z S N D C
```

ACKLEY	CAULFIELD	IMMATURE	POEMS
ACTORS	CHRISTMAS	LAVENDER	RADIO
ALLIE	DB	LUCE	SALINGER
ANTOLINI	ERNIE	MAURICE	SALLY
BAGS	FAILED	MORON	SIMMONS
BEANS	FENCING	MUSEUM	SPENCER
CAROUSEL	GALLAGHER	NOSE	STRADLATER
CASTLE	GLOVE	NUNS	SUNNY
CATCHER	GREEN	PHOEBE	TRAIN

CROSSWORD - *The Catcher in the Rye*

CROSSWORD CLUES - *Catcher in the Rye*

ACROSS
2. James; committed suicide
5. Roomed next to Holden at Pencey
6. Holden's brother in Hollywood
8. Holden lied to this boy's mother on the train
9. English teacher
12. The elevator operator who set up Holden with Sunny
14. Holden's condition in the rain watching Phoebe on the carousel
15. Shoulder movement indicating 'I don't care' or 'I don't know'
17. Way of saying goodbye; __-__!
19. Present singular of 'to be'
20. Closer
21. Holden's transportation to NY
23. Holden liked it because everything there stayed put
26. ___ City; Holden saw a show there
27. Student at Whooton; had a drink with Holden
28. Lillian; DB's old girlfriend
31. Bothersome person
33. Holden wrote Stradlater's composition about Allie's
34. Holden danced with Bernice et al in the ___ Room
36. Holden was kicked out of Pencey because he ___
38. Author

DOWN
1. Holden's dead brother
2. Holden watched Phoebe ride one
3. Enthusiasm; Holden didn't have any school -----
4. Test
5. Holden thought these people were the biggest phonies of all
7. Phoebe packed hers so she could go with Holden
10. An ____ man wants to die nobly for a cause
11. Little Shirley ____; record Holden bought Phoebe
13. ____ in the Rye
16. Walked
18. Narrator; Holden
20. Stradlater gave Holden a bloody one
22. Season to be jolly
23. Holden often calls people this name
24. Holden chatted with them at the sandwich bar
25. Color of ink writing on Allie's glove
29. Ponder; think over
30. Holden's theater date
31. Allie's glove had these written on it
32. Definite article
35. Faster than walk
37. Masculine personal pronoun

CROSSWORD ANSWER KEY - *The Catcher in the Rye*

						A			C	A	S	T	L	E		
				A	C	K	L	E	Y		A		P		X	
	D	B		C		L		E	R	N	I	E		A		
		A	N	T	O	L	I	N	I		O	R		M		B
		G		O		E		M	A	U	R	I	C	E	W	E	T
		S	H	R	U	G		M		S		T	A		C		A
			I	S		N	E	A	R	E	R		T	R	A	I	N
C	K			O	T		L			C		U		S
H	E	M	U	S	E	U	M		N		H		F			G
R	A	D	I	O		E		R		L	U	C	E		I		R
I			R			E		N		R		E			E
S	I	M	M	O	N	S		P	E	S	T		G	L	O	V	E
T		U		N		A		O		H			D			N
M		L		L	A	V	E	N	D	E	R					
F	A	I	L	E	D		L		M		U		H		
S					Y		S	A	L	I	N	G	E	R		

MATCHING QUIZ/WORKSHEET 1 - *The Catcher in the Rye*

___ 1. TRAIN   A. Holden's roommate at Pencey

___ 2. GLOVE   B. Holden wrote Stradlater's composition about Allie's

___ 3. BEANS   C. Holden's theater date

___ 4. NUNS   D. Holden's dead brother

___ 5. ALLIE   E. Holden was kicked out of Pencey because he ___

___ 6. SUNNY   F. Allie's glove had these written on it

___ 7. MUSEUM   G. Season to be jolly

___ 8. POEMS   H. Narrator; Holden

___ 9. SPENCER   I. The prostitute

___10. FAILED   J. Holden chatted with them at the sandwich bar

___11. ANTOLINI   K. Holden often calls people this name

___12. MORON   L. Holden's sister

___13. GREEN   M. Color of ink writing on Allie's glove

___14. PHOEBE   N. Author

___15. LAVENDER   O. Holden liked it because everything there stayed put

___16. CAULFIELD   P. English teacher

___17. SALINGER   Q. Holden's transportation to NY

___18. SALLY   R. Holden's history teacher

___19. CHRISTMAS   S. Holden danced with Bernice et al in the___ Room

___20. STRADLATER   T. Little Shirley ____; record Holden bought Phoebe

MATCHING QUIZ/WORKSHEET 2 - *The Catcher in the Rye*

___ 1. FENCING   A. Stradlater gave Holden a bloody one

___ 2. SUNNY   B. Holden wrote Stradlater's composition about Allie's

___ 3. ANTOLINI   C. Holden often calls people this name

___ 4. MUSEUM   D. Holden's theater date

___ 5. ERNIE   E. Color of ink writing on Allie's glove

___ 6. SALLY   F. Phoebe packed hers so she could go with Holden

___ 7. NOSE   G. Holden returned to school with the ___ team

___ 8. CATCHER   H. The prostitute

___ 9. CHRISTMAS   I. ___ City; Holden saw a show there

___ 10. CAULFIELD   J. Author

___ 11. RADIO   K. Holden liked it because everything there stayed put

___ 12. SIMMONS   L. ___ in the Rye

___ 13. MORON   M. English teacher

___ 14. CASTLE   N. Season to be jolly

___ 15. SALINGER   O. Lillian; DB's old girlfriend

___ 16. MAURICE   P. Holden's roommate at Pencey

___ 17. BAGS   Q. Narrator; Holden

___ 18. STRADLATER   R. Holden lied to this boy's mother on the train

___ 19. GREEN   S. The elevator operator who set up Holden with Sunny

___ 20. GLOVE   T. James; committed suicide

KEY: MATCHING QUIZ/WORKSHEETS - *The Catcher in the Rye*

Worksheet 1	Worksheet 2
1. Q	1. G
2. B	2. H
3. T	3. M
4. J	4. K
5. D	5. R
6. I	6. D
7. O	7. A
8. F	8. L
9. R	9. N
10. E	10. Q
11. P	11. I
12. K	12. O
13. M	13. C
14. L	14. T
15. S	15. J
16. H	16. S
17. N	17. F
18. C	18. P
19. G	19. E
20. A	20. B

JUGGLE LETTER REVIEW GAME CLUE SHEET - *The Catcher in the Rye*

SCRAMBLED	WORD	CLUE
SEUUMM	MUSEUM	Holden liked it because everything there stayed put
OMNSISM	SIMMONS	Lillian; DB's old girlfriend
OVLEG	GLOVE	Holden wrote Stradlater's composition on Allie's glove
LYLAS	SALLY	Holden's theater date
TACRSO	ACTORS	Holden though these people were the biggest phonies of all
ECLU	LUCE	Student at Whooton; had a drink with Holden
AITNR	TRAIN	Holden's transportation to NY
IFNECGN	FENCING	Holden returned to school with the _____ team
ENOS	NOSE	Stradlater gave Holden a bloody one
REDVEANL	LAVENDER	Holden danced with Bernice et al in the _____ Room
HBEOEP	PHOEBE	Holden's sister
EFALI	FAILED	Holden was kicked out of Pencey because he
UFADECIL	CAULFIELD	Narrator; Holden
YECKLA	ACKLEY	Roomed next to Holden at Pencey
NASBE	BEANS	Little Shirley _____; record Holden bough Phoebe
SCLEAT	CASTLE	James; committed suicide
LININATO	ANTOLINI	English teacher
REISGLAN	SALINGER	Author
ACHTMRISS	CHRISTMAS	Season to be jolly
EMSOP	POEMS	Allie's glove had these written on it
LIELA	ALLIE	Holden's dead brother
NNUYS	SUNNY	The prostitute
UEAMRIC	MAURICE	The elevator operator who set up Holden with Sunny
CEHTCRA	CATCHER	_____ in the Rye
REAMUMIT	IMMATURE	An _____ man wants to die nobly for a cause
GBSA	BAGS	Phoebe packed hers so she could go with Holden
CRESPEN	SPENCER	Holden's history teacher
RNEEI	ERNIE	Holden lied to this boy's mother on the train
SNUN	NUNS	Holden chatted with them at the sandwich bar
SLUERCAO	CAROUSEL	Holden watched Phoebe ride one
LHRGELGAA	GALLAGHER	Jane; Holden's former girlfriend

VOCABULARY RESOURCE MATERIALS

VOCABULARY WORD SEARCH - *The Catcher in the Rye*

All words in this list are associated with *The Catcher in the Rye* with an emphasis on the vocabulary words chosen for study in the text. The words are placed backwards, forward, diagonally, up and down. The included words are listed below.

```
A R I S T O C R A T I C P E D A G O G I C A L N
Q G C H L S A N S N A W S B R I P T N D Y O D M
S J R D Y S I I F P P M Z N P L G T I K U E C Z
H J Z O P B O E A B L A S E S B I R L S T I B Y
S V N Y P E R C H A Y W M I S M T J E A T Y R D
G U G V G I I N U T A P S U A U V G C S V O T J
Z F O R O T N Q S N A O O T P K Q I I H S I Y O
S H U R Y R Y G K R T I E G S T T D T L O E S K
T O I L E D Q Y R I T L H K B S A N U T D T S H
B T J H J T L D L N Y V L B I S A P I X R G Q V
Y H T Q F N S A E R R A L H S L M N Y A F W M K
Q N F Y M W H I P C C H P C A O G W C S J G M B
R R N H C L C W O I C O U H C O L I L M L O M B
P M S W H S X M N B S Z C M C N Z W J E D H Z M
Y U N A N I M O U S G N B N B E M H P N N N F L
X D G O P M R D T M O F I H D L L X A R S Y Y T
P A C I F I S T E N O G R A P H E R F R O C K K
```

ARISTOCRATIC	EXPEL	LAVISH	RASPY
ATHEIST	FROCK	LOUSE	SADISTIC
BLASE	GROPING	NONCHALANT	SOPHISTICATED
BOISTEROUS	HALITOSIS	OSTRACIZED	STENOGRAPHER
BOURGEOIS	HUMBLE	PACIFIST	SWANKY
CAPACITY	INCOGNITO	PEDAGOGICAL	UNANIMOUS
COMPULSORY	INFERIORITY	PUTRID	CONSCIENTIOUS
INTIMATELY	QUALMS	DIGRESSES	IRONICAL
RANDOM			

VOCABULARY CROSSWORD - *The Catcher in the Rye*

VOCABULARY CROSSWORD CLUES - *Catcher in the Rye*

ACROSS
1. Phoebe packed hers so she could go with Holden
3. One who opposed the use of force under any circumstances
8. Opposite of fast
10. Required; must be done
13. Get back at; get ----
14. Reaching blindly
17. A person who believes there is no God
21. Grating
22. Getting pleasure from inflicting pain on others
24. Past tense of 'to say'
25. Won't is a contraction for will ---
26. Shunned; excluded; left out
28. Stradlater gave Holden a bloody one
29. Little Shirley ____; record Holden bought Phoebe
31. Hunting ---
34. A person regarded as mean or contemptible
35. Holden's dead brother
36. Holden wrote Stradlater's composition about Allie's
37. Noisy; unruly
39. Drive out by force
40. Of an upper class; distinguished
44. Present singular of 'to be'
45. The prostitute
46. Rambles; departs temporarily from the main topic
47. Thought
48. Holden was kicked out of Pencey because he ___
49. Unhappy face

DOWN
1. Smug; conventional; materialistic
2. Opposite of stop
3. Noise a balloon makes when it bursts
4. Green and red, for example
5. Coat; cloak
6. Sneaky
7. Expensive and showy
9. Generous or liberal in giving or spending
10. Ability to contain, absorb, receive and hold
11. Attentive to duty; diligent
12. Privately; personally; very closely
15. Meaning opposite of what is expressed
16. A person skilled in taking shorthand
18. Lowly; unpretentious
19. In disguise
20. Exams
23. Feelings of doubt
27. Holden's brother in Hollywood
30. Holden chatted with them at the sandwich bar
32. Hit with the flat of one's hand
33. Unnaturally focused on one thought or object
36. Color of ink writing on Allie's glove
37. Having done something so much as to be bored by it
38. Roomed next to Holden at Pencey
39. Holden lied to this boy's mother on the train
41. ___ City; Holden saw a show there
42. Holden's transportation to NY
43. Clenched hand; Maurice hit Holden with his ----
44. Bothers

VOCABULARY CROSSWORD ANSWER KEY - *The Catcher in the Rye*

VOCABULARY WORKSHEET 1 - *The Catcher in the Rye*

___ 1. Bursting of blood vessels
    a. Frequently   b. Humble   c. Hemorrhages   d. Bourgeois

___ 2. Required; must be done
    a. Louse   b. Unanimous   c. Compulsory   d. Humble

___ 3. Held the attention of; captivated
    a. Exhibitionist   b. Fascinated   c. Halitosis   d. Frock

___ 4. A person regarded as mean or contemptible
    a. Groping   b. Sophisticated   c. Lavish   d. Louse

___ 5. Smug; conventional; materialistic
    a. Sadistic   b. Bourgeois   c. Frock   d. Raspy

___ 6. Ability to contain, absorb, receive and hold
    a. Capacity   b. Blase   c. Groping   d. Expel

___ 7. A person skilled in taking shorthand
    a. Compulsory   b. Bourgeois   c. Aristocratic   d. Stenographer

___ 8. Rotten
    a. Putrid   b. Expel   c. Lavish   d. Conscientious

___ 9. Showing a lack of concern; casually indifferent
    a. Nonchalant   b. Louse   c. Aristocratic   d. Swanky

___10. Shunned; excluded; left out
    a. Incognito   b. Ostracized   c. Sophisticated   d. Pedagogical

___11. Of an upper class; distinguished
    a. Bourgeois   b. Aristocratic   c. Swanky   d. Random

___12. Generous or liberal in giving or spending
    a. Lavish   b. Qualms   c. Capacity   d. Fascinated

___13. Rambles; departs temporarily from the main topic
    a. Sophisticated   b. Unscrupulous   c. Digresses   d. Lavish

___14. Privately; personally; very closely
    a. Intimately   b. Louse   c. Bourgeois   d. Humble

___15. Getting pleasure from inflicting pain on others
    a. Digresses   b. Frock   c. Swanky   d. Sadistic

___16. Attentive to duty; diligent
    a. Conscientious   b. Frock   c. Random   d. Stenographer

___17. Expensive and showy
    a. Raspy   b. Incognito   c. Swanky   d. Boisterous

___18. Noisy; unruly
    a. Boisterous   b. Fascinated   c. Groping   d. Incognito

___19. Bad smelling breath
    a. Halitosis   b. Pacifist   c. Intimately   d. Humble

___20. Characteristic of teaching or teachers
    a. Aristocratic   b. Hemorrhages   c. Ironical   d. Pedagogical

VOCABULARY WORKSHEET 2 - *The Catcher in the Rye*

___ 1. COMPULSORY A. Mutual; equivalent; interchangeable

___ 2. LAVISH B. One who opposed the use of force under any circumstances

___ 3. SOPHISTICATED C. Showing or based on total agreement

___ 4. HUMBLE D. Meaning opposite of what is expressed

___ 5. PEDAGOGICAL E. Grating

___ 6. RASPY F. Smug; conventional; materialistic

___ 7. RECIPROCAL G. Generous or liberal in giving or spending

___ 8. STENOGRAPHER H. Strong feelings of inadequacy

___ 9. INTIMATELY I. Characteristic of teaching or teachers

___10. CAPACITY J. Worldly wise; refined

___11. QUALMS K. Ability to contain, absorb, receive and hold

___12. BOURGEOIS L. A person who believes there is no God

___13. UNANIMOUS M. A person skilled in taking shorthand

___14. IRONICAL N. Feelings of doubt

___15. OSTRACIZED O. Required; must be done

___16. FREQUENTLY P. Lowly; unpretentious

___17. ATHEIST Q. Privately; personally; very closely

___18. PACIFIST R. Having done something so much as to be bored by it

___19. BLASE S. Shunned; excluded; left out

___20. INFERIORITY T. Often

KEY: VOCABULARY WORKSHEETS - *The Catcher in the Rye*

Worksheet 1	Worksheet 2
1. C	1. O
2. C	2. G
3. B	3. J
4. D	4. P
5. B	5. I
6. A	6. E
7. D	7. A
8. A	8. M
9. A	9. Q
10. B	10. K
11. B	11. N
12. A	12. F
13. C	13. C
14. A	14. D
15. D	15. S
16. A	16. T
17. C	17. L
18. A	18. B
19. A	19. R
20. D	20. H

VOCABULARY JUGGLE LETTER REVIEW GAME CLUES - *The Catcher in the Rye*

SCRAMBLED	WORD	CLUE
NORMDA	RANDOM	Haphazardly; without careful choice; by chance
TMENTLIIYA	INTIMATELY	Privately; personally; very closely
TTRAICSAOCRI	ARISTOCRATIC	Of an upper class; distinguished
CSSITDAI	SADISTIC	Getting pleasure from inflicting pain on others
CTAYAPCI	CAPACITY	Ability to contain, absorb, receive and hold
TDPIRU	PUTRID	Rotten
FOTIIYRNIRE	INFERIORITY	Strong feelings of inadequacy
RNGOPIG	GROPING	Reaching blindly
MLUASQ	QUALMS	Feelings of doubt
YSPAR	RASPY	Grating
ZDCETORSIA	OSTRACIZED	Shunned; excluded; left out
KOCRF	FROCK	Coat; cloak
NAWKYS	SWANKY	Expensive and showy
CCLOREPAIR	RECIPROCAL	Mutual; equivalent; interchangeable
OUELS	LOUSE	A person regarded as mean or contemptible
ACGDALIPEGO	PEDAGOGICAL	Characteristic of teaching or teachers
SNETXIIOBIHIT	EXHIBITIONIST	One who likes to show off and get attention
ACNHLTNNAO	NONCHALANT	Showing a lack of concern; casually indifferent
EGROETNPHRSA	STENOGRAPHER	A person skilled in taking shorthand
YUOMSCOPLR	COMPULSORY	Required; must be done
IPFAICTS	PACIFIST	One who opposed the use of force under any circumstances
ACSDIPITTHEOS	SOPHISTICATED	Worldly wise; refined
IGEUSRBO	BOURGEOIS	Smug; conventional; materialistic
SLUNOUSPCUUR	UNSCRUPULOUS	Having no moral code; unprincipled
LYENFREQUT	FREQUENTLY	Often
LSEAB	BLASE	Having done something so much as to be bored by it
ILHVAS	LAVISH	Generous or liberal in giving or spending
OBSUEROSIT	BOISTEROUS	Noisy; unruly
SIATTHE	ATHEIST	A person who believes there is no God
DAINTFASCE	FASCINATED	Held the attention of; captivated
OKCRF	FROCK	Coat; cloak
ICSNTESCOIUNO	CONSCIENTIOUS	Attentive to duty; diligent
ISSCTIAD	SADISTIC	Getting pleasure from inflicting pain on others
LEBUMH	HUMBLE	Lowly; unpretentious
RREHSMEOHGA	HEMORRHAGES	Bursting of blood vessels
SIAHITOSL	HALITOSIS	Bad smelling breath
COLANRII	IRONICAL	Meaning opposite of what is expressed

www.ingramcontent.com/pod-product-compliance
Lightning Source LLC
Chambersburg PA
CBHW051418070526
44584CB00023B/3480